Especially for

..............................................................

From

..............................................................

Date

..............................................................

# Choose
# PRAYER

## 3-MINUTE DEVOTIONS
## FOR WOMEN

BARBOUR BOOKS
An Imprint of Barbour Publishing, Inc.

© 2018 by Barbour Publishing, Inc.

ISBN 978-1-68322-398-6

All rights reserved. No part of this publication may be reproduced or transmitted for commercial purposes, except for brief quotations in printed reviews, without written permission of the publisher.

Churches and other noncommercial interests may reproduce portions of this book without the express written permission of Barbour Publishing, provided that the text does not exceed 500 words or 5 percent of the entire book, whichever is less, and that the text is not material quoted from another publisher. When reproducing text from this book, include the following credit line: "From *Choose Prayer: 3-Minute Devotions for Women*, published by Barbour Publishing, Inc. Used by permission."

Scripture quotations marked NIV are taken from the Holy Bible, New International Version®. NIV®. Copyright © 1973, 1978, 1984, 2011 by Biblica, Inc.™ Used by permission. All rights reserved worldwide.

Scripture quotations marked KJV are taken from the King James Version of the Bible.

Scripture quotations marked NKJV are taken from the New King James Version®. Copyright © 1982 by Thomas Nelson, Inc. Used by permission. All rights reserved.

Scripture quotations marked MSG are from *THE MESSAGE*. Copyright © by Eugene H. Peterson 1993, 1994, 1995, 1996, 2000, 2001, 2002. Used by permission of NavPress Publishing Group.

Scripture quotations marked NLT are taken from the *Holy Bible*. New Living Translation copyright© 1996, 2004, 2015 by Tyndale House Foundation. Used by permission of Tyndale House Publishers, Inc. Carol Stream, Illinois 60188. All rights reserved.

Scripture quotations marked ESV are from The Holy Bible, English Standard Version®, copyright © 2001 by Crossway Bibles, a publishing ministry of Good News Publishers. Used by permission. All rights reserved.

Scripture quotations marked NASB are taken from the New American Standard Bible, © 1960, 1962, 1963, 1968, 1971, 1972, 1973, 1975, 1977, 1995 by The Lockman Foundation. Used by permission.

Scripture quotations marked RSV are taken from the Revised Standard Version of the Bible, copyright 1946, 1952 [2nd edition, 1971] by the Division of Christian Education of the National Council of the Churches of Christ in the United States. Used by permission. All rights reserved.

Scripture quotations marked AMP are taken from the Amplified® Bible, © 2015 by The Lockman Foundation. Used by permission.

Scripture quotations marked NCV are taken from the New Century Version of the Bible, copyright © 2005 by Thomas Nelson, Inc. Used by permission. All rights reserved.

Readings are excerpted from: *365 Encouraging Verses of the Bible for Women, Daily Wisdom for Women: 2013 and 2014 Devotional Collections, How God Grows a Woman of Wisdom*, and *How God Grows a Woman of Prayer*. Copyright © Barbour Publishing. Inc. All rights reserved.

Published by Barbour Books, an imprint of Barbour Publishing, Inc., 1810 Barbour Drive, Uhrichsville, Ohio 44683, www.barbourbooks.com

*Our mission is to inspire the world with the life-changing message of the Bible.*

Member of the
Evangelical Christian
Publishers Association

Printed in the United States of America.

# Choose Prayer!

These devotions were written especially for those moments when you need a little reminder that every single day should be filled with prayer. Just three tiny minutes is all you'll need to refresh and revitalize your spirit.

- Minute 1: Read the day's Bible verse and reflect on its meaning.

- Minute 2: Read the devotional and think about its application for your life.

- Minute 3: Pray.

Although these devotionals aren't meant as a tool for deep Bible study, they can be a touch point to keep you grounded and focused on God, the One who listens to your every prayer. May every moment you spend with this book be a blessing!

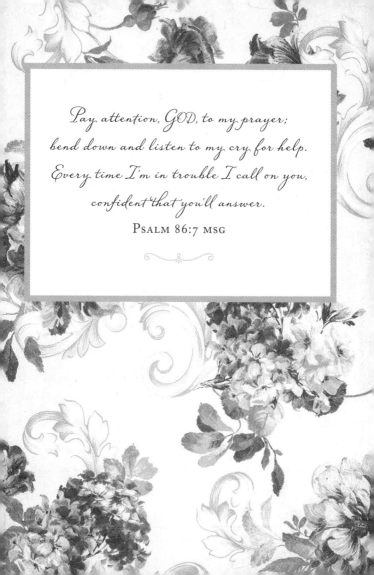

Pay attention, GOD, to my prayer;
bend down and listen to my cry for help.
Every time I'm in trouble I call on you,
confident that you'll answer.

PSALM 86:7 MSG

# Prayerful Consideration

*Trust in the LORD with all your heart
and lean not on your own understanding;
in all your ways submit to him,
and he will make your paths straight.*
PROVERBS 3:5–6 NIV

Have you ever had to make a decision, but didn't know what to do? As Christians, we have a reliable resource for counsel. When decision-making poses a threat to our serenity and peace, Proverbs 3:5–6 provides sound advice.

God provides the solution to decision-making with a promise—namely, if we take all our concerns to God, He will direct our paths. When we're tempted to act on our own wisdom, the Lord tells us to stop, reflect, and prayerfully consider each matter. He gives us uncomplicated advice for our major and not-so-major decisions. The question is, will we listen? That's the most important decision of all.

*Often, Lord, I run on ahead of You and make
decisions on my own. Help me to remember that even
with small decisions I need to seek Your will. Amen.*

# Every Step of the Way

*Never stop praying.*
1 Thessalonians 5:17 nlt

Several passages in the Bible tell us clearly that God listens to us when we pray. He hears every word and is compassionate. All we have to do is share our concerns with Him and wait faithfully for what He will provide.

God wants to be involved in our daily routines. He wants to hear from us and waits for us. God never promised an easy life to Christians. If we will allow Him, though, God will be there with us every step of the way. All we need to do is to come to Him in prayer. With these three simple words from 1 Thessalonians 5:17, our lives can be fulfilling as we live to communicate with our Lord.

*Father, when I pray, remind me that prayer is*
*not only about talking to You, but also about listening*
*to You. Open my heart to Your words. Amen.*

## A Bold Request

*When they had crossed, Elijah said to Elisha,
"Tell me, what can I do for you before I am
taken from you?" "Let me inherit a double
portion of your spirit," Elisha replied.*
2 Kings 2:9 NIV

What a bold request.

Elijah filled the role of leader, prophet, and miracle worker. Why would Elisha want the heavy responsibilities and difficulties involved in this type of work? He did not ask to have a larger ministry than Elijah—he was only asking to inherit what Elijah was leaving and to be able to carry it on.

What might God give us if we asked boldly for the impossible? God deeply desires to bless us. If our hearts line up with His will and we stay open to His call, He will surprise us. God takes the ordinary and through His power transforms our prayers into the extraordinary—even double-portion requests.

*Bless me, Lord. When my heart aligns with Your
will and when I ask for the impossible, bless me. Show me
beyond my expectations that You are my God. Amen.*

# He Will Answer

*I waited patiently for the LORD;*
*and he inclined unto me, and heard my cry.*
*He brought me up also out of an horrible pit.*

PSALM 40:1–2 KJV

David found himself trapped in a "horrible pit" with no apparent way out, and he cried loudly to the Lord to rescue him. Then he waited. It took time for God to answer. David undoubtedly learned more patience in the process and probably had to endure doubts, wondering if God cared about the dilemma he was in.

Even Jeremiah didn't always get immediate answers to prayer. One time he and some Jewish refugees were in a dire situation and were desperate to know what to do. Yet after Jeremiah prayed, the Lord took ten days to answer (Jeremiah 42:7). But the answer *did* come. . .in time.

Today we sometimes find ourselves in a "horrible pit" as well, and we pray desperately for God to bring us up out of it. He will. We often just need to be patient.

*Why is patience so hard? It's because Your timing is perfect and beyond my understanding. Help me to be patient with You, God. I know that You will answer me. Amen.*

# Stillness

*Be still, and know that I am God.*
PSALM 46:10 NKJV

David wrote, "Meditate within your heart on your bed, and be still" (Psalm 4:4 NKJV). Many of us have lost the ability to meditate on God. We either tell ourselves that meditation is something only Buddhist monks do, or else we cry out frantic prayers while distracted by the careening roller coaster of life. When we lie down in bed at night, instead of meditating calmly and trusting in God, we fret and toss and turn.

When we learn to trust that God can protect us and work out our problems, then we can lie down peacefully and sleep (Psalm 4:8). That same trust gives us the strength to face our days with confidence.

*Dear God, quiet my mind. Remove from it all the worldly thoughts that come between You and me. Create stillness within me, and turn my thoughts toward You. Amen.*

# Thy Will Be Done

*He went away a second time and prayed, "My Father,
if it is not possible for this cup to be taken away
unless I drink it, may your will be done."*
MATTHEW 26:42 NIV

Jesus didn't just ask this just once—He made this request three times in Matthew 26. These red-letter prayers reveal the 100 percent human side of Jesus.

In one of His darkest hours, Jesus was overwhelmed with trouble and sorrow. He asked God for something that God would not provide. But Jesus, perfect and obedient, ended His prayers by saying, *"Your will be done."*

When we face our darkest hours, will we follow Jesus' example? Can we submit to God's perfect will, focusing on how much He loves us—even when His will doesn't match ours?

*I wonder why You refuse when I ask for what
I think is right. But Your knowledge is greater than
my understanding. So, Thy will be done, God,
Thy perfect will be done. Amen.*

# God's Great Mercy

*"We do not make requests of you because we are righteous, but because of your great mercy."*
**DANIEL 9:18 NIV**

When Daniel "understood from the Scriptures, according to the word of the LORD given to Jeremiah the prophet, that the desolation of Jerusalem would last seventy years" (Daniel 9:2 NIV), he prayed a long prayer of confession for his people, who had sinned so badly and persistently against God that He had allowed heavy punishment to fall upon them. And in the midst of that prayer, Daniel uttered one of the great truths of scripture, the verse we know now as Daniel 9:18.

Let's understand, with Daniel, that we bring absolutely nothing to God. But let's also know, like Daniel, that in God's great mercy, He chooses to hear, love, and forgive us.

*Oh Mighty God, Your great mercy is beyond my understanding. I have nothing to bring You, yet in my sinfulness You hear me, love me, and forgive me. Thank You, Father. Amen.*

## God Already Knows

*"As soon as you began to pray, a word
went out, which I have come to tell you,
for you are highly esteemed."*
DANIEL 9:23 NIV

In the middle of pouring out his heart to God one day, Daniel's prayer is interrupted by the appearance of the angel Gabriel. Bringing insight and understanding (v. 22), Gabriel's message contains the interesting concept that in the instant that Daniel began to pray, the answer was already on its way.

Before Daniel got past his salutation, God knew Daniel's heart and had already set in motion the response to Daniel's unfinished prayer.

As He did for Daniel, God knows our needs even before we give voice to them in prayer. We can rest in the knowledge that even before the words leave our lips, God has already heard them, and He has already answered them.

*Thank You, God, for answering my prayers.
Before the words leave my lips, You already have
the answer. How great You are, God! I praise You. Amen.*

# *Be Anxious for Nothing*

---

*Be anxious for nothing, but in everything by
prayer and supplication, with thanksgiving,
let your requests be made known to God.*
**PHILIPPIANS 4:6 NKJV**

"Be anxious for nothing" sounds like great advice, but at times most of us have the feeling that it only works for highly mature saints and is not practical for the average Christian.

Yet the key to making it work is found in the same verse: we can "be anxious for nothing" if we are continually taking those problems to God in prayer, thanking Him for solving past problems, and trusting Him to work the current situation out. Praying about things, of course, shouldn't keep us from doing what God inspires us to do to solve the problems. But we should trust and pray instead of fretting and worrying.

*Father, anxiety makes me weary. Today I ask You to take all my problems and work them out for my good. Show me the way, Lord, and I will obey You. Amen.*

# Beyond Words. . .to the Heart

*And so the Lord says, "These people say they are mine. They honor me with their lips, but their hearts are far from me. And their worship of me is nothing but man-made rules learned by rote."*

ISAIAH 29:13 NLT

From God's perspective, the actions of our hearts speak louder than our words. And if our worship consists of mindlessly repeating words and going with the flow, we are missing out on connecting with a God who fiercely loves us and desires to be in an unscripted relationship with us.

This verse carries a sobering reminder that God looks beyond the words of our mouths and considers the heart that utters them. Creeds and prayers are familiar ways to connect with God and serve as wonderful reminders of His steadfast character. The next time an opportunity arises to recite from memory, consider how to bring the well-known words to life in a new and fresh understanding—spoken from the heart.

*Father, when I read the Bible I will savor each word and consider its meaning. And when I pray a familiar prayer, I will pray from my heart. Amen.*

# According to His Purpose

*With this in mind, we constantly pray for you, that our God may make you worthy of his calling, and that by his power he may bring to fruition your every desire for goodness and your every deed prompted by faith.*

2 THESSALONIANS 1:11 NIV

God's sovereignty and our free will clash in a glorious kaleidoscope of grace in the second letter to the Thessalonians.

Here, Paul prayed for the church at Thessalonica, that God would make them worthy of His calling. God calls; then God makes them deserving of that calling.

Elsewhere, Paul commanded believers to *live* lives worthy of God and His calling (Ephesians 4:1). Our effort, our choice.

Here, Paul prays that God will fulfill *our* purposes and actions prompted by our faith.

But God is the One who calls us "according to His purpose" (Romans 8:28 NIV; 2 Timothy 1:9). In fact, Paul goes so far as to say that call is "irrevocable" (Romans 11:29 NIV).

Let's rest in the fact that all the things we live and plan and believe, God will fulfill for us.

*I believe You will fulfill the plans You have for me. Right now, You are enlightening me to Your will. Thank You, Father! Amen.*

## Call on Him in Faith

*"Call to me and I will answer you and tell you great
and unsearchable things you do not know."*
JEREMIAH 33:3 NIV

Jeremiah 33:3 teaches that if we pray to God, He will answer us with wisdom. In the King James Version of the Bible, the word *pray* is used more than five hundred times. God wants us to pray. When we call on Him in prayer, we know that He hears us (1 John 5:15).

Proverbs 2:6 (NASB) says, "For the LORD gives wisdom; from His mouth come knowledge and understanding." God knows us fully, and He is able to direct us in wisdom and guide us through the works of His Holy Spirit.

Just as God gave Jeremiah wisdom when he prayed, He will do the same for you if you call on Him in faith (James 1:5–6).

*God, I need Your help. I've sought counsel for my
problem, and still I'm not sure what to do. But You know!
Please, God, guide me with Your wisdom. Amen.*

# No Limits

*Great is our Lord, and of great power:*
*his understanding is infinite.*
PSALM 147:5 KJV

When you're praying for wisdom in a complex or desperate situation, fix this thought firmly in your mind: You may have no clue as to the right answer, but God certainly does! His understanding is without end.

At times, we don't understand why God allows us to go through troubled times, but He certainly knows—and He cares deeply for each one of us. He not only knows every star by name, but He knows *your* name, too.

Psalm 147:5 is one of the most powerful scriptures in the Bible. When we meditate deeply on its words, they can fill our minds with peace and assurance.

*God, who am I among all the stars in the universe?*
*But You know their names, and You know*
*mine, too! You know me, You understand*
*me, and that brings me peace. Amen.*

# Prayer Schedule

*Seven times a day I praise you*
*for your righteous laws.*
PSALM 119:164 NIV

The Bible tells us to pray without ceasing. A fixed-hour prayer ritual is called "praying the hours" or the "daily office." Hearts and minds turn toward God at set times. We make an effort to create a space in our busy lives to praise God and express our gratitude throughout the day.

We can create any kind of prayer schedule. Each stoplight we pass, the ring of the alarm on our watches, or a pause during television commercials can all serve as simple reminders to pray. We can be alert during the day for ways God protects and guides us.

Seven moments a day—to thank the Lord for all the moments of our lives.

*Sometimes I forget to pray; busyness gets in the way.*
*But I can change that! I will set aside specific times*
*throughout my day to pray and praise You, Lord. Amen.*

# *Praying Great Prayers*

*And the sun stood still, and the moon stayed,
until the people had avenged themselves
upon their enemies.*

JOSHUA 10:13 KJV

As Joshua prepared his men to fight, God promised him that He had already delivered the enemy into Israel's hand and that none of them would stand before the Israelites (v. 8). After they had smashed the overwhelming foe in battle and watched God drop bombs of hailstones on them, Joshua asked God to stop the clock. The sun and moon paused, and Joshua's men had another day of light to erase the menace.

The longest day in history was also a day for believing in the Lord for victory. Joshua went against the combined armies of five kings because he believed the Lord's promise, and he saw God fight for him. In that spirit, he prayed a great prayer. May we be emboldened to pray great prayers when we see the Lord following through in our lives!

*God, fight for me! I believe in victory over my troubles
and my enemies. Their words and deeds pierce me like
arrows, but with Your great love You protect me. Amen.*

*The Very Best*

---

*"But if you remain in me and my words
remain in you, you may ask for anything
you want, and it will be granted!"*
JOHN 15:7 NLT

Wow! Really? Is that true?

As silly as this may sound, there are some who assume
that they have license to treat God as a concierge of some
kind, who is standing by to rush to fulfill their every request.

As we present our requests to God, we need to realize
that He knows what is best for us and that we should never
demand "our way." We must not forget the first part of
John 15:7 that says, "If you remain in me and my words
remain in you." This should clearly tell us that our first
desires need to be that God's will is done.

Since God only wants to give us the very best, and
He knows how to make that happen, why would we pray
for anything else?

*Father, I say, "Thy will be done!"
You know best. I want what You want for me,
even if it's not what I ask for. Amen.*

# When Words Fail Me

*Before a word is on my tongue you, LORD,*
*know it completely.*
**PSALM 139:4 NIV**

Sometimes Christians feel so overwhelmed by their needs or by the greatness of God that they simply can't pray. When the words won't come, God helps to create them. Paul says in Romans 8:26 (NLT), "And the Holy Spirit helps us in our weakness. For example, we don't know what God wants us to pray for. But the Holy Spirit prays for us with groanings that cannot be expressed in words."

God hears your prayers even before you pray them. When you don't know what to say and the words won't come, you can simply ask God to help you by praying on your behalf.

*Dear God, I'm grateful today that*
*in my silence You still hear me. Amen.*

# Your Best Friend

*God is faithful, who has called you into fellowship
with his Son, Jesus Christ our Lord.*
1 CORINTHIANS 1:9 NIV

When do you pray? How often do you call on God? Where do you talk to Him?

When, where, or how we talk to God is of little importance to the Savior. We can converse with the Lord while driving down the street, walking through the park, or standing at the kitchen sink. We can ask for His help with the most insignificant or even the biggest decisions. Our concerns are His concerns, too, and He desires for us to share our heartfelt thoughts with Him.

Fellowshipping with God is talking to our best Friend, knowing He understands and provides help and wisdom along life's journey. It's demonstrating our faith and trust in the One who knows us better than anyone.

*Lord, remind me to talk to You anytime, anywhere.
I know that as I pray, You will talk to me too. Amen.*

# Call on Me

―❦―

*"Call on me in the day of trouble;*
*I will deliver you, and you will honor me."*
PSALM 50:15 NIV

When God says He wants us to call Him, He means it.
He must lean closer, bending His ear, waiting, longing for
the sound of His name coming from our lips. He stands
ready to deliver us from our troubles or at least to carry
us through them safely.

While He doesn't always choose to fix things with a
snap of His fingers, we can be assured that He will see us
through to the other side of our troubles by a smoother
path than we'd travel without Him. He's waiting to help
us. All we have to do is call.

*Dear Father, I'm so glad I can call on You*
*anytime, with any kind of trouble. Amen.*

# Pray Persistently

*Rejoice always, pray continually, give thanks in all circumstances; for this is God's will for you in Christ Jesus.*
1 Thessalonians 5:16–18 niv

The Gospel of Luke tells about a widow who had an ongoing dispute with an enemy. The woman was stubborn and determined to win, and she refused to give up her dispute until a judge ruled in her favor. Many times she went to the judge demanding, "Give me justice!"

Jesus used this story to teach His followers about persistent prayer. He said, "Learn a lesson from this unjust judge. Even he rendered a just decision in the end. So don't you think God will surely give justice to his chosen people who cry out to him day and night?" (Luke 18:6–7 nlt).

When Christians pray, it shows not only their faith in God but also their trust in His faithfulness toward them. In His time, the Lord will come and bring justice to His people.

*Dear God, help me to remain faithful and not grow weary in prayer. Amen.*

# Pray Instead of Plotting

*"Pray that the LORD your God
will show us what to do and where to go."*
**JEREMIAH 42:3 NLT**

However bleak your situation seems, God hasn't forgotten you. Philippians 4:6–7 (NLT) says, "Don't worry about anything; instead, pray about everything. Tell God what you need, and thank him for all he has done. Then you will experience God's peace, which exceeds anything we can understand. His peace will guard your hearts and minds as you live in Christ Jesus."

Jeremiah 42:3 echoes this statement. It urges believers to pray for guidance instead of setting out with a preconceived notion of how the day (or month or decade) will turn out.

When you begin to worry that you don't have what it takes to meet life's demands, remember that you don't have to—because God does.

*Jesus, thank You for Your presence and the peace You
so freely give. Help me to pray before I worry,
categorize, or strategize. Amen.*

*Just in Time*

---

*Therefore let us [with privilege] approach the throne of grace [that is, the throne of God's gracious favor] with confidence and without fear, so that we may receive mercy [for our failures] and find [His amazing] grace to help in time of need [an appropriate blessing, coming just at the right moment].*

HEBREWS 4:16 AMP

As believers, our lives become exciting when we wait on God to direct our paths, because He knows what is best for us at any given moment. His plans and agenda are never wrong.

Once we fully realize He knows best and turn our lives over to the Spirit for direction, we can allow God to be in charge of calendar; His timing is what is paramount.

When chomping at the bit for a job offer or for a proposal, His timing might seem slow. "Hurry up, God!" we groan. But when we learn to patiently wait on His promises, we will see the plans He has for us are more than we dared hope—or dream. God promises to answer us; and it never fails to be just in time.

*Lord, I want Your perfect will in my life.*
*Help me learn to wait upon You. Amen.*

# Who God Hears

*The LORD is far from the wicked,*
*but he hears the prayers of the righteous.*
PROVERBS 15:29 NLT

When the righteous call God's name, He hears. Though none of us is righteous on our own, we can claim righteousness through Jesus Christ. He alone is righteous, and He covers us like a cloak. When we call on God, He sees the righteousness that covers us through Christ and recognizes us as His children. He leans over and listens carefully to our words because we belong to Him. He loves us.

Next time it seems like God isn't listening, perhaps we should examine our hearts. Have we pushed God away? Have we accepted the price His Son, Jesus Christ, paid on our behalf? If not, we can't claim righteousness. If we have, we can trust that He's never far away. He hears us.

*Dear Father, thank You for making me*
*righteous through Your Son, Jesus. Amen.*

# Worry vs. Prayer

*Don't worry about anything; instead,*
*pray about everything. Tell God what you*
*need, and thank him for all he has done.*
PHILIPPIANS 4:6 NLT

The Bible tells us not to worry about *anything*. In the book of Matthew, we are reminded that if God cares for the birds of the air, providing them with food as they need it, He is certain to take care of His children! But if we give up worrying, what will we do with all the time we spent being anxious? Exchange it for time in prayer. Go before God with your concerns. Cast all your cares on Him, for He promises to care for you. Tell God what you need and thank Him in advance for what He will do. God will always provide. He will always show up. He does not want you to worry.

*Lord, replace my worry time with prayer time.*
*It is in Jesus' name that I come before You now,*
*presenting You with my requests. Thank You*
*for Your provision in my life. Amen.*

# The Gift of Prayer

*First of all, then, I urge that petitions (specific requests),*
*prayers, intercessions (prayers for others) and*
*thanksgivings be offered on behalf of all people. . .*
*This [kind of praying] is good and acceptable and*
*pleasing in the sight of God our Savior.*
1 TIMOTHY 2:1, 3 AMP

Perhaps the absolute greatest gift one person can give
to another doesn't come in a box. It can't be wrapped or
presented formally, but instead it is the words spoken to
God for someone—the gift of prayer.

When we pray for others, we ask God to intervene and
to make Himself known to them. We can pray for God's
plan and purpose in their lives. We can ask God to bless
them or protect them. You can share with them that you are
praying for them or do it privately without their knowledge.
Who would God have you give the gift of prayer to today?

*Lord, thank You for bringing people to my heart and mind*
*who need prayer. Help me to pray for the things that they*
*need from You in their lives. Show me how to give the gift*
*of prayer to those You would have me pray for. Amen.*

*At All Times*

*Pray in the Spirit at all times
with all kinds of prayers.*
EPHESIANS 6:18 NCV

God wants to be included in our days. He wants to walk and talk with us each moment. Imagine if we traveled through the day with our children or our spouse, but we only spoke to them between 6:15 and 6:45 a.m! Of course we'd never do that to the people we care about. God doesn't want us to do that to Him, either.

God wants to travel the journey with us. He's a wonderful Companion, offering wisdom and comfort for every aspect of our lives. But He can only do that if we let Him into our schedules, every minute of every day.

*Dear Father, thank You for always being there
to listen. Remind me to talk to You about
everything, all the time. Amen.*

## Praying Together

*For where two or three are gathered together
in my name, there am I in the midst of them.*
MATTHEW 18:20 KJV

Of all the passages in the Bible that emphasize the importance of gathering for worship and prayer, this one stands out. It is short and sweet and to the point. Why should we gather together to pray with other Christians? Because when we do, *God shows up!* The Lord is in our midst.

As you gather with other Christians in your church or even in your family, God is honored. He loves to listen to the hearts and voices of His children unified in prayer. He will be faithful to answer according to His perfect will.

*Father, thank You for the promise that where we gather in Your name, there You will be also. Help me never to give up the practice of praying with fellow believers. Amen.*

# Before You Ask

*"Seek the Kingdom of God above all else,*
*and live righteously, and he will give*
*you everything you need."*
MATTHEW 6:33 NLT

In the Lord's Prayer, Jesus teaches His followers how to pray. He begins, "Our Father in heaven, may your name be kept holy. May your Kingdom come soon. May your will be done on earth, as it is in heaven" (Matthew 6:9–10 NLT). First, Jesus honors God's holiness. Next, He shows faith in God's promise of reigning over the earth and redeeming His people. Then He accepts God's perfect will. Praise, faith, and acceptance come before asking. Jesus reminds believers to honor God first, put God's will second, and pray for their own needs third. His prayer begins with God and ends with Him: "For thine is the kingdom, and the power, and the glory, for ever. Amen," (Matthew 6:13 KJV).

Bring your requests to God. Ask specifically and confidently, but remember Jesus' model—put God first in your prayers.

*Dear God, I praise You. My faith rests in You,*
*and I accept whatever Your will is for my life. Amen.*

# Ask in Faith

*But when you ask God, you must believe
and not doubt. Anyone who doubts is like a wave
in the sea, blown up and down by the wind.*

JAMES 1:6 NCV

What does it mean to ask God for something *in faith*?
Does it mean we believe that He *can* grant our requests?
That He *will* grant our requests? Exactly what is required
to prove our faith?

There is no secret ingredient that makes all our longings
come to fruition. The secret ingredient, if there is one, is faith
that God is who He says He is. It's faith that God is good
and will use our circumstances to bring about His purpose
and high calling in our lives and in the world.

When we don't get the answers we want from God,
it's okay to feel disappointed. He understands. But we must
never doubt His goodness or His motives. We must stand
firm in our belief that God's love for us will never change.

*Dear Father, I know that You are good and that You love
me. I know Your love for me will never change, even when
my circumstances are hard. Help me cling to Your love,
even when You don't give the answers I want. Amen.*

# Powerful Praying

*Therefore confess your sins to each other and pray
for each other so that you may be healed. The prayer
of a righteous person is powerful and effective.*

JAMES 5:16 NIV

When we have God's approval, when we live with integrity and faith, He listens to us. But when we consistently make poor choices and disregard God's guidance, He may not take our prayers as seriously.

Oh, He will never take His love from us, no matter what. And He will always listen when we ask for help out of our sin. But if we want our prayers to hold extra power, we need to live righteously. When we have God's approval on our lives, we can also know we have God's ear about all sorts of things. When we walk in God's will, we have access to God's power.

*Dear Father, I want my prayers to be powerful
and effective. Help me to live in a way
that pleases You. Amen.*

# A Good Morsel

*Taste and see that the LORD is good;*
*blessed is the one who takes refuge in him.*
PSALM 34:8 NIV

The world gives the idea to nonbelievers that God isn't worth a taste. The world emphasizes a self-focus, while the Lord says put others before self and God before all. In reality, walking and talking with God is the best thing you can do for yourself. As you walk with God, learning to pray and lean on Him and operate in His will, you are storing up treasures for yourself in heaven. In the world, you are demonstrating the love of Christ and being an influence to make others want a taste of the Lord.

Like so many foods that are good for us, all it requires is that first taste, a tiny morsel, which whets the appetite for more of Him. Then you can be open to all the goodness, all the fullness of the Lord.

*Lord, fill my cup to overflowing with Your love,*
*so that it pours out of me in a way that makes*
*others want what I have. Amen.*

# Start Your Day with God

*In the morning, LORD, you hear my voice; in the morning*
*I lay my requests before you and wait expectantly.*
**PSALM 5:3 NIV**

How can you start your day with God even if you haven't
gotten up hours earlier for devotions? As you wake up in
the morning, thank the Lord for a new day. Ask Him to
control your thoughts and attitude as you make the bed.
Thank Him for providing for you as you toast your bagel.
Ask that your self-image be based on your relationship with
Christ as you get dressed and brush your teeth. Continue
to pray as you drive to work or school. Spend time in His
Word throughout the day. End your day by thanking Him
for His love and faithfulness.

God wants a constant relationship with you, and He
is available and waiting to do life with you twenty-four
hours a day.

*Dear Lord, thank You for the gift of a new day.*
*Help me be aware of Your constant*
*presence in my life. Amen.*

# Our Prayer Calling

*Then she [Anna] lived as a widow to the age of eighty-four.*
*She never left the Temple but stayed there day and night,*
*worshiping God with fasting and prayer.*
LUKE 2:37 NLT

Have you ever felt useless to the kingdom of God? Do you think you have little to offer, so you offer little? Consider the eighty-four-year-old widow, Anna. She stayed at the temple worshipping God through prayer and fasting. That was her calling, and she was committed to prayer until the Lord ushered her home.

We need not pray and fast like this dedicated woman did. (In fact, for health reasons, fasting is not always an option.) Yet we are all called to pray. We can pray right where we are, regardless of our age, circumstances, or surroundings. Like Anna, it's our calling.

*Lord, please remind me of the calling of prayer*
*on my life, despite my circumstances. Amen.*

# Hand Holders

*As long as Moses held up his hands, the Israelites were winning, but whenever he lowered his hands, the Amalekites were winning. When Moses' hands grew tired, they took a stone and put it under him and he sat on it. Aaron and Hur held his hands up. . .so that his hands remained steady till sunset. So Joshua overcame the Amalekite army.*

EXODUS 17:11–13 NIV

How do you view your pastor? Do you see him as the cheerleader of your congregation, trying to motivate them to be better Christ-followers? Perhaps the teacher? Maybe even the ultimate decision-maker? The truth is, some pastors feel that they are expected to be all things to all people and to do it with perfection.

Our verse today shows that Moses was an ordinary (but called) person trying to do a huge job by himself. No one could be expected to hold his hands up for the duration of a battle. He needed help. One way we can help our pastors in the work they have been given is by the power of consistent prayer for them personally, for their families, and for their ministry.

*Father, our pastors are precious to us. Remind us to keep our pastors in prayer. It is one way we can hold their hands high to You. Amen.*

# God's Good and Perfect Will

*For this reason, since the day we heard about you,
we have not stopped praying for you. We continually
ask God to fill you with the knowledge of his will through
all the wisdom and understanding that the Spirit gives.*

**Colossians 1:9 NIV**

The apostle Paul reminded the Colossians that he was continuously praying for them to be filled with the knowledge of God's will. Christians have received the Holy Spirit as their Counselor and Guide. Those who do not have a personal relationship with Christ are lacking the Spirit, and thus, they are not able to discern God's will for their lives. Always take advantage of the wonderful gift that you have been given. If you have accepted Christ as your Savior, you also have the Spirit. One of the greatest things about the Holy Spirit is that He helps us to distinguish God's call on our life from the other voices of the world. Pray that God will reveal His good and perfect will for your life.

*God, help me to draw upon the wonderful resources
that I have as a Christian. Help me, through the
power of the Holy Spirit, to know Your will. Amen.*

# Prayer Touches God

*He [Cornelius] was a devout, God-fearing man...*
*He gave generously to the poor and prayed regularly to God.*
ACTS 10:2 NLT

In the book of Acts, a centurion named Cornelius received a vision from God. Though a Gentile, this man loved God, praying and fasting regularly. While he prayed, an angel of the Lord told Cornelius that God heard and honored his prayers. Accordingly, God instructed the centurion to go talk to Peter, God's servant.

Jesus takes note of a praying, giving heart like Cornelius had. Denominations mean little, while a contrite, teachable spirit touches God. Cornelius was a good, God-fearing man who needed to hear about salvation through Christ. So God honored his prayers and led him to the preacher—while teaching the preacher a thing or two at the same time.

Have you hesitated to share your faith with someone you think unseemly or beyond your realm of comfort? Begin now. Look what happened when Peter did.

*Father, forgive me for my self-righteousness.*
*Open the way for me to witness to whomever*
*You have prepared to hear the Gospel. Amen.*

## Listening Closely

*I will listen to what God the LORD says.*
PSALM 85:8 NIV

In today's hurried world, with all of the surrounding noise, it's easy to ignore the still, small voice nudging us in the right direction. We fire off requests, expect microwave-instant answers, and get aggravated when nothing happens. Our human nature demands a response. How will we know what to do/think/say if we do not listen? As the worship song "Speak to My Heart" so beautifully puts, when we are "yielded and still" then He can "speak to my heart."

Listening is a learned art, too often forgotten in the busyness of a day. The alarm clock buzzes, we hit the floor running, toss out a prayer, maybe sing a song of praise, grab our car keys, and are out the door. If only we'd slow down and let the heavenly Father's words sink into our spirits, what a difference we might see in our prayer life. This day, stop. Listen. See what God has in store for you.

*Lord, how I want to surrender and seek Thy will.*
*Please still my spirit and speak to me. Amen.*

# A Declaration of Dependence

*"Sacrifice thank offerings to God. . .and call on me in the day of trouble; I will deliver you, and you will honor me."*

PSALM 50:14–15 NIV

Most of us value our relationships, whether they are family, friends, or coworkers. We like being in relationships with those who offer love, commitment, and trust because we feel valued. Perhaps not so ironically, today's verse reveals that God wants the same things from us. He wants thankful, trusting, and faithful children, people whom He can delight in and who can delight in Him.

As our heavenly Father, He wants to help us, especially in times of trouble. That dependency on Him recognizes that everything we have comes from Him. The practical way to depend on Him comes through an honest, consistent lifestyle of prayer, where we offer ourselves and our needs. Through prayer, we draw near to Him and get to know Him better. In doing that, we'll become the thankful, trusting, and faithful children He desires.

*Father, thank You for loving me so much that You are interested in every facet of my life. I commit to bring everything to You in prayer and acknowledge that I am dependent on You for my provision. Amen.*

58

# Pray about Everything

*The LORD directs the steps of the godly.*
*He delights in every detail of their lives.*
PSALM 37:23 NLT

The Bible says that the Lord delights in every detail of His children's lives. And no matter how old a believer is, they are and always will be God's child.

Adult prayers don't have to be well ordered and formal. God loves hearing His children's voices, and no detail is too little or dull to pray about. Tell God that you hope the coffeehouse will have your favorite pumpkin-spice latte on their menu. Ask Him to give you patience as you wait in line. Thank Him for how wonderful that coffee tastes! Get into the habit of talking with Him all day long, because He loves you and delights in all facets of your life.

*Dear God, teach me to pray about everything*
*with childlike innocence and faith. Amen.*

# He Cares for You

*"You have seen what I did to the Egyptians,*
*and how I carried you on eagles' wings,*
*and brought you to Myself."*
EXODUS 19:4 AMP

Often we feel deserted. As though God doesn't hear our prayers. And we wait. When Moses led the children of Israel out of Egypt toward the promised land, God directed him to go the distant way, lest the people turn back quickly when things became difficult. The people placed their hope in an almighty God and followed His lead. When they thirsted, God gave water. When they hungered, He sent manna. No need was unmet.

If God can do this for so many, you can rest assured that He will care for you. He knows your needs before you even ask. Place your hope and trust in Him. He is able. He's proven Himself, over and over. Read the scriptures and pray to the One who loves you. His care is infinite. . . and He will never disappoint you.

*Heavenly Father, I know You love me*
*and hear me. I bless Your holy name. Amen.*

## Earnest Prayer

*"[If] My people, who are called by My Name,*
*humble themselves, and pray and seek (crave,*
*require as a necessity) My face and turn from their*
*wicked ways, then I will hear [them] from heaven,*
*and forgive their sin and heal their land."*

2 CHRONICLES 7:14 AMP

The Amplified Bible specifies how believers are to humble themselves and pray. We are to "seek, crave, and require of necessity" God's face.

We should *seek* God relentlessly.

*Crave.* Our desire for God's presence in our lives ought to be strong and irresistible.

*Necessity.* Our hearts need God for survival. He is our one and only true necessity.

When you pray, call out to God with your whole heart. Prayer must be more than an afterthought to close each day, as eyelids grow heavy and sleep wins the battle. Seek God. Crave and require His face. Turn toward Him. He stands ready to hear, to forgive, and to heal.

*Lord, be my greatest desire,*
*my craving, my all. Amen.*

# Fix Your Thoughts on Truth

*Fix your thoughts on what is true, and honorable,
and right, and pure, and lovely, and admirable.
Think about things that are excellent
and worthy of praise.*
PHILIPPIANS 4:8 NLT

In a world loaded with mixed messages and immorality of every kind, it becomes increasingly difficult to have pure thoughts and clear minds. What can a believer do to keep her mind set on Christ? Replace the negative message with a positive message from God's Word.

Dig through the scriptures and find truth from God's Word to combat the false message that you're struggling with. Write them down and memorize them. Here are a few to get started:

God looks at my heart, not my outward appearance (1 Samuel 16:7).

I am free in Christ (1 Corinthians 1:30).

I am a new creation. My old self is gone! (2 Corinthians 5:17).

Pray for the Lord to replace the doubts and negativity with His words of truth.

*Lord God, please help me set my mind
and heart on You. Amen.*

# Praying for All People

*I urge, then, first of all, that petitions, prayers, intercession and thanksgiving be made for all people—for kings and all those in authority, that we may live peaceful and quiet lives in all godliness and holiness. This is good, and pleases God our Savior, who wants all people to be saved and to come to a knowledge of the truth.*
1 TIMOTHY 2:1–4 NIV

Whether we like the person who is in office or not, God commands us to pray for those He placed in authority over us. In ancient times, this could have meant praying for those who hated Christians and were possibly plotting harm to them. Even today, as issues concerning Christ-followers emerge, we are called to pray for all people, including those with whom we don't see eye to eye politically. Today's verse reminds us that doing this is good and pleasing to the Lord.

*Gracious Lord, thank You for the admonition to pray for all people, including those whom we disagree with. All people are precious to You, Lord. Please help me put my own feelings aside and be obedient in praying for all those in authority. Amen.*

# Wait Expectantly

*Listen to my voice in the morning, Lord.*
*Each morning I bring my requests to*
*you and wait expectantly.*
PSALM 5:3 NLT

Why would the psalmist say he waits *expectantly* upon praying to the Lord each morning? Perhaps it is because he had seen God answer prayers time and time again!

Think about a baby who cries out in the night. The baby learns to expect a parent to come and lift him out of the crib to provide comfort, food, or a dry diaper. Babies in orphanages often stop crying. No one comes when they cry. There is no use. The expectation for rescue and provision wanes. Your heavenly Father is eager and ready to meet with you when you come before Him in prayer. The Bible tells us that His eyes are always roaming across the earth, searching for those who are after His own heart (2 Chronicles 16:9). When you lift your requests to the Sovereign God, rest assured that He is ready to answer. Wait expectantly!

*Lord, thank You that You are a God who hears*
*my prayers, and answers. Thank You in advance*
*for all that You are doing in my life. Amen.*

# Public Prayer

So I bow in prayer before the Father from whom every
family in heaven and on earth gets its true name.
EPHESIANS 3:14–15 NCV

A heartfelt prayer offered in public glorifies God and
allows others to feel His presence; however, the scriptures
include a warning about public prayer. Matthew 6:5 advises
people not to act like the hypocrites who want to be seen
and heard praying just to show how pious and religious
they are. Public prayer must be sincere and directed toward
God and not toward others.

Every day, Christians gather together, bow their
heads, and pray publicly in churches, at prayer groups, at
funeral and memorial services, in restaurants before meals,
and even around school flagpoles. They pray sincerely,
sometimes silently and sometimes aloud, setting aside
the world and entering into God's presence.

Are you shy about praying in public? Don't be. Step
out in faith, bow your head, and pray like God is the only
One watching.

*Heavenly Father, I am not ashamed to bow my head
and be in Your presence wherever I go. Amen.*

# Call unto Me

*Look to the LORD and his strength;*
*seek his face always.*
PSALM 105:4 NIV

David, the psalmist, had no choice but to rely on the Lord as he fled his enemies. The lyrics of the Psalms remind us he was no stranger to loss and fear. Yet he cried unto the Lord. His words in Psalm 105 encourage us to remember what He has done before. Paul sat in the pits, literally, and sang songs of praise. While we might not be in dire straits like those men, we certainly have problems, and we can read scripture to see how the Lord has worked to have confidence that He is near.

Let us work to seek His face always. Know that the Lord cares about each detail of your life, and nothing is a secret or a surprise to Him. Reach for the best and expect results. It might require a time of waiting, but His answers are always unsurpassed.

*Almighty Father, thank You for loving me so well.*
*In times when I fear, help me fall into*
*Your embrace. Amen.*

# The Power of Prayer

*Confess your sins to each other and pray for each other so that you may be healed. The earnest prayer of a righteous person has great power and produces wonderful results.*
**JAMES 5:16 NLT**

Have you given your heart to Jesus? If you have accepted Him as your Savior, you have taken on the *righteousness* of Christ. Certainly you are not perfect. In your humanity, you still sin and fall short. But God sees you through a Jesus lens! And so, your prayers reach the ears of your heavenly Father.

Pray often. Pray earnestly. Pray without ceasing. Pray about everything. Prayer changes things. Look at Jesus' example of prayer during His time on earth. He went away to quiet places such as gardens to pray. He prayed in solitude. He prayed with all His heart. If anyone was busy, it was the Messiah! But Jesus always made time to pray. We ought to follow His example. Prayer changes things.

*Lord, help me to believe in the power of prayer and to make time for it daily. Amen.*

## Pray for Others

---

*I urge, then, first of all, that petitions, prayers,*
*intercession and thanksgiving be made for all people.*
1 TIMOTHY 2:1 NIV

Intercessory prayer is a divine act of love and service. It requires persistence, patience, and faith in God. Christians should intercede for family and friends, their country, government leaders, their pastors, the Church, the poor, the sick, the community in which they live, their enemies, and especially for those who are not saved. Wherever there is a need, Christians should pray.

The Bible holds many examples of intercessory prayer. Look for them as you read the scriptures. Discover how God's people prayed and the great changes those prayers made.

Intercessory prayer is just as important today as it was in Timothy's time. It draws believers nearer to God and provides them with a powerful way to help others. Whom will you pray for today?

*Heavenly Father, guide me as I pray for*
*others. Help me to pray for them faithfully,*
*patiently, and persistently. Amen.*

# Renew Your Strength

*But those who wait for the Lord. . .will gain new strength and renew their power; they will lift up their wings [and rise up close to God] like eagles [rising toward the sun].*
ISAIAH 40:31 AMP

Andrew Murray was a South African writer, teacher, and Christian pastor in the late 1900s who captured the heart of prayer with these words about Jesus: "While others still slept, He went away to pray and to renew His strength in communion with His Father. He had need of this; otherwise He would not have been ready for the new day. The holy work of delivering souls demands constant renewal through fellowship with God."

Each day you give a part of yourself to that day—spiritually, emotionally, physically, financially, and socially. Within each of those areas of life, you need to refuel. Spiritually, the only way to recharge is a renewal that comes from God. Waiting for a fresh outpouring of His life-giving Spirit brings a newness and a fresh perspective on all the other areas of your life. Give your best each day by drawing on the strength of your heavenly Father.

*Heavenly Father, Your Word and prayer are strength to my soul. Renew me and pour Your life into me. Amen.*

# Stop, Breathe, Pray. . .and Repeat

*Do not be anxious about anything, but in every situation
. . .present your requests to God. And the peace of God,
which transcends all understanding, will guard
your hearts and your minds in Christ Jesus.*

PHILIPPIANS 4:6–7 NIV

Being a woman in these times is challenging. Many of us are working demanding jobs, managing our homes and crazy schedules, and taking care of children or aging parents. Often, we feel we don't have enough time to get everything done, let alone take care of ourselves properly. All of this creates stress and anxiety, which just makes many of these situations worse.

What can you do when it seems the world is falling down around your shoulders? Stop. Take a deep breath, and then settle your mind on Jesus. Give Him the situation, the harried thoughts, the worries. God says that we can take anything to Him in prayer! He will provide whatever we need, even the peace that will get us through the most difficult circumstances.

*Father God, we are thankful that we can take any worried
thought or situation to You in prayer. Help us to lay the
situation at Your feet and leave it there. Amen!*

# Focused Prayer

*Pray in the Spirit at all times and on every occasion.
Stay alert and be persistent in your prayers for
all believers everywhere.*
**EPHESIANS 6:18 NLT**

The Bible warns us to stay alert and to pray persistently. The key is to focus on Jesus even in the midst of the storm. If the captain of a ship or the pilot of a plane loses focus in the middle of a storm, it can be very dangerous for all involved. Our job as believers is to trust the Lord with the outcome and to remain deliberate and focused in our prayers.

The Bible does not say to pray when it is convenient or as a last resort. It does not say to pray just in case prayer might work or to add prayer to a list of other things we are trying. We are instructed in Ephesians to pray at *all* times and on *every* occasion. When you pray, pray in the Spirit. Pray for God's will to be done. Pray in the name of Jesus.

*Jesus, I set my eyes upon You, the Messiah,
my Savior, Redeemer, and Friend. Amen.*

# The Right Focus

*Turning your ear to wisdom and applying your heart
to understanding—indeed, if you call out for insight
and cry aloud for understanding, and if you look for
it as for silver and search for it as for hidden treasure,
then you will understand the fear of the LORD
and find the knowledge of God.*

PROVERBS 2:2–5 NIV

Even when you're looking in the right direction, you can still miss something because your focus is slightly off. This can be the challenge in our relationship with God. We can ask God a question and be really intent in getting the answer, only to find that His response to us was there all along—just not the answer we expected or wanted.

Frustration and stress can keep us from clearly seeing the things that God puts before us. Time spent in prayer and meditation on God's Word can often wash away the dirt and grime of the day-to-day and provide a clear picture of God's intentions for our lives. Step outside the pressure and into His presence, and get the right focus for whatever you're facing today.

*Lord, help me to avoid distractions
and keep my eyes on You. Amen.*

# Teach Me Your Paths

*Show me your ways, L*ORD*, teach me your paths.*
*Guide me in your truth and teach me, for you are*
*God my Savior, and my hope is in you all day long.*
PSALM 25:4–5 NIV

Hebrews 4:12 tells us that the scriptures are living and active. Just think about that for a moment. God's Word is alive! As busy women, it can be difficult to find the time to open the Bible and meditate on the message—but it's *necessary* if you want God to teach you His path for your life.

Instead of giving up on finding time for Bible reading, get creative. Download a free Bible app on your phone. Have a daily scripture reading and devotion emailed to you from heartlight.org. Jot down a few verses on a note card to memorize. There are many ways to get in the Word of God and be trained by it. Start today!

*Lord, I believe Your Word is living and active.*
*I want to know Your will for my life. Help me get in*
*Your Word more and understand Your plan for me. Amen.*

# Prayer and the Word Unlock the Door

*I pray that your hearts will be flooded with light so that
you can understand the confident hope he has given
to those he called—his holy people who are
his rich and glorious inheritance.*

EPHESIANS 1:18 NLT

Math is a language all its own. Unfortunately, many students struggle to learn that language. Sometimes they never understand it completely but retain just enough of the language to make it through required courses.

Your spiritual life is also a different language. God's ways are not the ways of this world. Often His ways of doing things are similar to learning a new language. Prayer can unlock the door to understanding God's Word and His design for your life. As you spend time with God in prayer asking for understanding of His Word, His truth will speak to you in a brand-new way. The Holy Spirit will help you unlock the secrets of His purpose and plan for your life.

*Heavenly Father, thank You for the Bible. Help me to
read it with understanding and come to know
You in a whole new way. Amen.*

74

# Pray for His Return

*The end of all things is near. Therefore be alert
and of sober mind so that you may pray.*
1 Peter 4:7 NIV

Around 600 BC, Jerusalem fell to the Babylonians. The Jews were exiled to Babylonia and held captive for seventy years. God told the prophet Jeremiah to tell His people to settle there and live normally. He said they should seek peace in the place in which they lived until He came back to get them (Jeremiah 29:4–7).

Today's Christians are similar to those Jews. They live normally in an evil world, seeking peace on earth while holding on to the promise of Jesus' return.

Paul wrote, "Brothers and sisters, whatever is true, whatever is noble, whatever is right, whatever is pure, whatever is lovely, whatever is admirable. . .think about such things. . . . And the God of peace will be with you" (Philippians 4:8–9 NIV).

May God's peace be with you today and every day until Jesus comes.

*Lord, may Your kingdom come and the
earth be filled with Your glory. Amen.*

# Pray for Christian Households

*When she speaks, her words are wise,*
*and she gives instructions with kindness.*
PROVERBS 31:26 NLT

In Christian households, children learn about God's love and faithfulness. Discipline is administered out of lovingkindness, not anger, and love is taught through the parents' example. It is a home in which Christlike wisdom is passed from generation to generation.

In Timothy's household (see 2 Timothy 1:5), he learned from his mother and grandmother's faith; and according to Paul, those seeds of faith grew in young Timothy and led him to become a servant of the Lord.

Whether you are married or single, have children or not, you can plant seeds of faith though your own Christian example and prayer. Pray for all children that they will grow up in godly homes, and pray for women everywhere that they will raise their children in Christian households and remain always faithful to God.

*Heavenly Father, shine Your light through me today*
*so that I might be an example to others. Amen.*

# Prayer Targets Selfishness

*Do nothing out of selfish ambition. . . . Rather, in humility value others above yourselves, not looking to your own interests but each of you to the interests of the others.*
PHILIPPIANS 2:3–4 NIV

This scripture discourages selfish ambition and encourages us to look to the interests of others. As believers, God expects us to take the high road. That means, despite someone's behavior, we are called to pray. Pray for her salvation; pray for God to work on her heart and mind; pray that when approached with the truth, she will receive it with a humble, open spirit.

God targets every heart with the arrow of His Word. It travels as far as the power of the One who thrust it on its course. Prayer, coupled with God's Word spoken to the unlovable, never misses the bull's-eye.

But we must first pray to see beyond the selfishness and view the needs behind it. When we do, God equips us to pray for others. Then the arrow of transformation is launched.

*Jesus, help me not only tolerate but also pray for the ones for whom You died. Amen.*

# How Long Has It Been?

*Trust in him at all times, you people;*
*pour out your hearts to him, for God is our refuge.*
PSALM 62:8 NIV

Has it been a long time since you've completely poured out your heart to God? Not just your everyday prayers for family and friends, but a complete and exhaustive outpouring of your heart to the Lord? Oftentimes we run to friends or spiritual counselors in times of heartache and trouble, but God wants us to pour out our hearts to Him first. He is our refuge, and we can trust Him to heal our hearts completely.

The next time you reach for the phone to call up a friend and share all of your feelings, stop and pray first. Share your heart with God and gain His perspective on your troubles. The God who created you knows you better than anyone. Let Him be your first point of contact in any situation.

*Heavenly Father, help me to trust that You are here*
*for me—to listen and to guide me. Give me wisdom*
*to make decisions that honor You. Amen.*

# Open the Eyes of Faith

*"Therefore I tell you, whatever you ask for in prayer,
believe that you have received it, and it will be yours."*
MARK 11:24 NIV

Have you ever prayed for something or someone, and God
seemed to turn a deaf ear? One woman prayed for her son's
salvation for seven years. Each day she knelt at the foot
of her tear-stained bed, pleading for her child. But God
seemed silent. Yet, what she failed to understand was that
the Lord had been working all along to reach her son in
ways unknown to her. And finally her son embraced the
Gospel through a series of life-changing circumstances.

The world says, "I'll believe it when I see it," while
God's Word promises, "Believe then see."

Someone once said, "The way to see by faith is to shut
the eye of reason." When we pray, rather than ask God
why our prayers remain unanswered, perhaps we should
ask the Lord to close our eyes so that we might see.

*Lord, I believe, even when my prayers go unanswered.
Instead, I know You are at work on my behalf. Amen.*

# A Refuge from Our Despair

*From the end of the earth I call to You when my heart is faint; lead me to the rock that is higher than I. For You have been a refuge for me, a tower of strength against the enemy. Let me dwell in Your tent forever; let me take refuge in the shelter of Your wings.*

PSALM 61:2–4 NASB

King David clung with tenacity to the fact that no matter how desperate his situation appeared, God was as immovable as a huge rock or boulder. Although David's trials may differ from yours, you too can use strong coping mechanisms.

First, David acknowledged that God remained all-powerful, despite life circumstances. And second, David looked back at God's past rescues. "O my God, my soul is in despair within me; therefore I remember You from the land of the Jordan, and the peaks of Hermon, from Mount Mizar. Deep calls to deep at the sound of Your waterfalls; all Your breakers and Your waves have rolled over me. The Lord will command His lovingkindness in the daytime; and His song will be with me in the night, a prayer to the God of my life" (Psalm 42:6–8 NASB).

*Lord, I search for a way through the torrents of despair. How precious is the knowledge that You hear and care. Amen.*

# Lay It at the Cross

*"Come to me, all you who are weary and burdened,
and I will give you rest. Take my yoke upon you and
learn from me. . .you will find rest for your souls.
For my yoke is easy and my burden is light."*
MATTHEW 11:28–30 NIV

Jesus gives us step-by-step guidance in how to place our difficulties and burdens at the foot of the cross. First, He invites us to come to Him; those of us who are weary and burdened just need to approach Jesus in prayer. Second, He exchanges our heavy and burdensome load with His easy and light load. Jesus gives us His yoke and encourages us to learn from Him. The word *yoke* refers to Christ's teachings, Jesus' *way* of living life. As we follow His teachings, we take his yoke in humility and gentleness, surrendering and submitting ourselves to His will and ways for our lives. Finally, we praise God for the rest He promises to provide us.

Do you have any difficulties in life, any burdens, worries, fears, relationship issues, finance troubles, or work problems that you need to "lay at the cross"? Jesus says, "Come."

*Lord, thank You for inviting me to come and exchange
my heavy burden for Your light burden. Amen.*

# Holy Spirit Prayers

*We do not know how to pray as we should, but the Spirit Himself intercedes for us with groanings too deep for words. . .He intercedes for the saints according to the will of God.*

ROMANS 8:26–27 NASB

Many times the burdens and troubles of our lives are too complicated to understand. It's difficult for us to put them into words, let alone know how to pray for what we need.

We can always take comfort in knowing that the Holy Spirit knows, understands, and pleads our case before the throne of God the Father. Our groans become words in the Holy Spirit's mouth, turning our mute prayers into praise and intercession "according to the will of God."

We can be encouraged, knowing that our deepest longings and desires, maybe unknown even to us, are presented before the God who knows us and loves us completely. Our names are engraved on His heart and hands. He never forgets us; He intervenes in all things for our good and His glory.

*Father, may I always be aware of the Holy Spirit's interceding on my behalf. Amen.*

## Ask for Directions

*The wicked in his proud countenance
does not seek God; God is in none of his thoughts.*
PSALM 10:4 NKJV

Do the laundry, wash the dishes, shop for groceries, cook dinner, work a full day, drive the kids to soccer practice—the list of a busy woman's duties goes on and on.

Somewhere along the way, we got the idea that it is wrong to ask for help. But you can't live the Christian life like that. It's impossible. If you don't ask for help, you won't stand a chance.

Women often tease that men would rather drive around lost for hours instead of stopping to ask for directions. But how often, in your own day, do you stop for a moment and ask the Father for directions? Jesus, knowing that He needed guidance from His Father, constantly sought His will by praying and asking for it. Instead of trying to find His own way through the day, Jesus fully depended on directions from above and actively pursued them.

*Jesus, forgive me for my pride and for not asking You for directions. Please show me the way to go and lead me in it. Help me to hear Your leading and then to follow it. Amen.*

# When Fear Paralyzes

*A young man was following Him, wearing nothing but
a linen sheet over his naked body; and they seized him.
But he pulled free of the linen sheet and escaped naked.
They led Jesus away to the high priest; and all the
chief priests and the elders and the scribes gathered
together. . . . The whole Council kept trying to obtain
testimony against Jesus to put Him to death,
and they were not finding any.*

MARK 14:51–55 NASB

Suddenly you awake at one in the morning to the sound
of the doorknob being turned and creaking boards. Your
heart leaps into your throat. What do you do?

When John Mark, the writer of this Gospel, learned
that Jesus had been captured by the Roman guards and a
trial was pending, he grabbed the sheet off his bed and ran to
observe the events himself.

We know John Mark escaped the threatening situation.
Yet Jesus Christ remained in the eye of the storm, well aware
of the situation yet in perfect sync with the Father. When
fear paralyzes, help is only a prayer away.

*Lord, I believe in all that You are,
both God and Man. Amen.*

# Talking to God

*One of his disciples said to him, "Lord, teach us to pray,*
*just as John taught his disciples." He said to them,*
*"When you pray, say: 'Father, hallowed be your name,*
*your kingdom come. Give us each day our daily bread.'"*
LUKE 11:1-3 NIV

Yes, God hears—and, although He knows what we need before we even ask Him, He *wants* us to pray. He even gave us instruction on how to pray. Our prayers don't have to be long or eloquent or even particularly organized. When Jesus taught His disciples to pray, the sample wasn't wordy. He simply taught the disciples to give God glory and to come to Him and ask for their daily needs.

But Luke 11 teaches us something beyond just an outline for prayer. The story shows clearly that if we ask God to teach us how to pray, He will. It's all part of the prayer—ask God to lead you, then speak to Him from the heart.

Let's make it a habit to pray every day. Like the saying goes, practice makes perfect.

*Dear God, teach me how to pray. Remind me that my*
*words don't have to be profound. You're just looking*
*for earnest thoughts from the heart. Amen.*

# Reach Out

*But people who aren't spiritual can't receive these truths
from God's Spirit. It all sounds foolish to them and
they can't understand it, for only those who are
spiritual can understand what the Spirit means.*

1 Corinthians 2:14 nlt

Unbelievers may feel confused trying to navigate the
unfamiliar territory of spiritual truth. They don't have the
ability to understand it because they don't have the Holy
Spirit as a teacher to guide them. The Bible may not make
sense to them, but don't be quick to judge. Hope isn't lost!

God likely has placed unbelievers in your life that
He wants you to reach out to. Share your faith with them
in words and actions they can understand. Pray the Lord
opens their hearts to receive Jesus as Lord and Savior.
Then the Holy Spirit will dwell with them, giving them
the ability to comprehend spiritual truth. Pray that these
lost "tourists" will find Jesus soon!

*Dear Lord, help me not judge those who don't
know You. Instead, I pray that You intercede
to show them the way. Amen.*

# *Vocalizing a Prayer*

*"And when you are praying, do not use meaningless repetition as the Gentiles do, for they suppose that they will be heard for their many words."*
MATTHEW 6:7 NASB

If you can remember the acrostic ACTS, you'll have an excellent formula for prayer: Adoration, Confession, Thanksgiving, and Supplication.

As we come before the Lord we first need to honor Him as Creator, Master, Savior, and Lord. Reflect on who He is and praise Him. And because we're human we need to confess and repent of our daily sins. Following this we should be in a mode of thanksgiving. Finally, our prayer requests should be upheld. My usual order for requests is self, family members, and life's pressing issues. Keeping a prayer journal allows for a written record of God's answers.

Your prayers certainly don't have to be elaborate or polished. God does not judge your way with words. He knows your heart. He wants to hear from You.

*Lord, Your Word says that my prayers rise up to heaven like incense from the earth. Remind me daily to send a sweet savor Your way! Amen.*

# Answered Prayer

*Delight yourself in the Lord;*
*and He will give you the desires of your heart.*
PSALM 37:4 NASB

Note the first part of Psalm 37:4: "Delight yourself in the Lord." A woman who truly delights herself in the Lord will naturally have the desires of her heart—because her heart desires only God and His will.

Our Father takes no pleasure in the things of this world—things that will all wither and die. Neither should we.

So what pleases God? He loves it when we witness for Him, live right, and instruct others in His Word. If those are things that we also truly desire, won't He grant us the "desires of our heart" and let us see people brought into the kingdom? Won't we have a life rich in spiritual growth?

*Lord, please help me see where my desires are not in line with Your will—so that the things that I pursue are only and always according to Your own desires. Amen.*

# So, Talk!

*"No one can come to Me unless the Father who sent
Me draws him [giving him the desire to come to Me];
and I will raise him up [from the dead] on the last day."*
JOHN 6:44 AMP

Fortunately for us human beings, God isn't easily offended.
He is deeply committed to holding up His end of our
relationship, and He doesn't want us to hide anything from
Him. He already knows every thought we have, anyway.
Why not talk to Him about those thoughts?

Every concern we have, every little thing that's good,
bad, or ugly.

Our Father always wants to talk. In fact, the very
impulse to pray originates in God. In his book *The Pursuit
of God*, author A. W. Tozer wrote, "We pursue God because,
and only because, He has first put an urge within us that
spurs us to the pursuit."

So, talk!

*Lord God, it boggles my mind that You want to hear
from me. And often! Your Word says that I can call out
Your name with confidence. That You will answer me!
Today, Lord, I give You praise, honor, and glory—
and my heart's deepest longings. Amen.*

# Submitting to His Will

*"Your kingdom come, your will be done,
on earth as it is in heaven."*
MATTHEW 6:10 NIV

Many times submitting to God's will requires letting go of something we covet. We may be called to walk away from a relationship, a job, or a material possession. At other times, God may ask us to journey down a path we would not have chosen. Venturing out of our comfort zone or experiencing hardship is not our desire.

Embracing God's love enables us to submit to His will. God not only loves us immensely, but He desires to bless us abundantly. However, from our human perspective, those spiritual blessings may be disguised. That is why we must cling to truth. We must trust that God's ways are higher than ours. We must believe that His will is perfect. We must hold fast to His love. As we do, He imparts peace to our hearts, and we are able to say with conviction, "Your will be done."

*Dear Lord, may I rest secure in Your unconditional love.
Enable me to trust You more. May I desire that
Your will be done in my life. Amen.*

# When God Redecorates

*God is the builder of everything.*
HEBREWS 3:4 NIV

God—the renovator of hearts—doesn't work cautiously. When He begins renovations, He removes (or allows the removal of) all existing supports. Maybe that "support" is health—ours or a loved one's. Maybe it's our savings. Maybe it's something else. Our lives, as we know them, crash. We hurt. We don't know how we can go on.

But God knows. If we let Him, He'll replace the temporary supports we'd relied on—health, independence, ability, you name it—with eternal spiritual supports like faith, surrender, and prayer. Those supports enable us to live a life of true freedom, one abounding with spiritual blessing.

*Lord, I am tempted to cling to the supports I've erected. When my life crashes, I'm tempted to despair. Please help me to be still and place my trust in You, the great builder of all lives. Amen.*

## Life Preservers

*My comfort in my suffering is this:*
*Your promise preserves my life.*
**PSALM 119:50 NIV**

In the difficulties of life, God is our life preserver. When we are battered by the waves of trouble, we can expect God to understand and to comfort us in our distress. His Word, like a buoyant life preserver, holds us up in the bad times.

But the life preserver only works if you put it on *before* your boat sinks. To get into God's life jacket, put your arms into the sleeves of prayer and tie the vest with biblical words. God will surround you with His love and protection—even if you're unconscious of His presence. He promises to keep our heads above water in the storms of living.

*Preserving God, I cling to You as my life preserver.*
*Keep my head above the turbulent water of caregiving*
*so I don't drown. Bring me safely to the shore. Amen.*

# Board God's Boat

*Then, because so many people were coming and going that they did not even have a chance to eat, he said to them, "Come with me by yourselves to a quiet place and get some rest."*
MARK 6:31–32 NIV

The apostles ministered tirelessly—so much so, they had little time to eat. As they gathered around Jesus to report their activities, the Lord noticed that they had neglected to take time for themselves. Sensitive to their needs, the Savior instructed them to retreat by boat with Him to a solitary place of rest where He was able to minister to them.

Often we allow the hectic pace of daily life to drain us physically and spiritually, and in the process, we deny ourselves time alone to pray and read God's Word. Meanwhile, God patiently waits.

So perhaps it's time to board God's boat to a quieter place and not jump ship!

*Heavenly Father, in my hectic life I've neglected time apart with You. Help me to board Your boat and stay afloat through spending time in Your Word and in prayer. Amen.*

# *Is Anyone Listening?*

> *"And I will ask the Father, and He will give you another Helper (Comforter, Advocate, Intercessor—Counselor, Strengthener, Standby), to be with you forever."*
>
> JOHN 14:16 AMP

The Greek translation for "comfort" is *paraklesis* or "calling near." When we are called near to someone, we are able to hear his or her whisper. It is this very picture scripture paints when it speaks of the Holy Spirit. God sent the Spirit to whisper to us and to offer encouragement and guidance, to be our strength when all else fails. When we pray—when we tell God our needs and give Him praise—He listens. Then He directs the Spirit within us to speak to our hearts and give us reassurance.

Our world is filled with noise and distractions. Look for a place where you can be undisturbed for a few minutes. Take a deep breath, lift your prayers, and listen. God will speak—and your heart will hear.

> *Dear Lord, I thank You for Your care.*
> *Help me to recognize Your voice*
> *and to listen well. Amen.*

# Answered Knee-Mail

*The prayer of a righteous person is
powerful and effective.*
**JAMES 5:16 NIV**

The concept of the power of prayer is familiar, but sometimes we forget what it means. Prayer is a powerful tool for communicating with God, an opportunity to commune with the Creator of the universe. Prayer is not something to be taken lightly or used infrequently. Yet, in the rush of daily life, we often lose sight of God's presence. Instead of turning to Him for guidance and comfort, we depend on our own resources.

But prayer isn't just a way to seek protection and guidance; it's how we develop a deeper relationship with our heavenly Father. We can access this power anywhere. We don't need a Wi-Fi hotspot or a high-speed modem. We just need to look up. He's connected and waiting.

*Father, thank You for being at my side all the time.
Help me to turn to You instantly, in need
and in praise. Amen.*

# What Is Your Request?

*And pray in the Spirit on all occasions with all kinds
of prayers and requests. With this in mind,
be alert and always keep on praying.*
EPHESIANS 6:18 NIV

Be patient. What we may view as a non-answer may simply
be God saying, "Wait" or "I have something better for you."
He *will* answer. Keep in mind that His ways are not our
ways, nor are His thoughts our thoughts.

God knows what He's doing, even when He allows
trials in our lives. We might think that saving a loved one
from difficulty is a great idea—but God, in His wisdom,
may decide that would be keeping them (or us) from an
opportunity for spiritual growth. Since we don't know all
of God's plans, we must simply lay our requests before Him
and trust Him to do what is right. He will never fail us!

*Father God, here are my needs. I lay them at Your feet,
walking away unburdened and assured that You
have it all under control. Thank You! Amen.*

# Put On a Happy Face

*He restoreth my soul: he leadeth me in the paths
of righteousness for his name's sake.*
PSALM 23:3 KJV

Be encouraged. The Lord has promised He hears our pleas
and knows our situations. He will never leave us. He will
guide us through our difficulties and beyond them. In
*Streams in the Desert*, Mrs. Charles E. Cowman states,
"Every misfortune, every failure, every loss may be transformed. God has the power to transform all misfortunes
into 'God-sends.'"

Today we should turn our thoughts and prayers toward
Him. Focus on a hymn or a praise song and play it in your
mind. Praise chases away the doldrums and tips your lips
up in a smile. With a renewed spirit of optimism and hope
we can thank the Giver of all things good. Thankfulness to
the Father can turn our plastic smiles into real ones, and
as the psalm states, our souls will be restored.

*Father, I'm down in the dumps today.
You are my unending source of strength.
Gather me in Your arms for always. Amen.*

# Hold On!

*Let us not become weary in doing good, for at the proper
time we will reap a harvest if we do not give up.*
GALATIANS 6:9 NIV

When Elijah fled for his life in fear of Jezebel's wrath,
depression and discouragement tormented him. Exhausted,
he prayed for God to take his life, and then he fell asleep.
When he awoke, God sent an angel with provisions to
strengthen his weakened body. Only then was he able
to hear God's revelation that provided the direction and
assistance he needed.

God hears our pleas even when He seems silent. The
problem is that we cannot hear Him because of physical
and mental exhaustion. Rest is key to our restoration.

Just when the prophet thought he could go on no
longer, God provided the strength, peace, and encouragement to continue. He does the same for us today. When
we come to the end of our rope, God ties a knot. And like
Elijah, God will do great things in and through us, if we
will just hold on.

*Dear Lord, help me when I can no longer help myself.
Banish my discouragement and give me the rest and
restoration I need so that I might hear Your voice. Amen.*

# Peace through Prayer

*Be anxious for nothing, but in everything by prayer
and supplication, with thanksgiving, let your requests
be made known to God; and the peace of God,
which surpasses all understanding, will guard
your hearts and minds through Christ Jesus.*

PHILIPPIANS 4:6–7 NKJV

There are days when thankfulness doesn't come naturally or easily. These are valley days—in the hospital room, at the graveside, or when we are distraught about a relationship or work issue. It is in these times that the Father wants us to give Him our burdens through prayer. It seems impossible to be thankful for the pain, the confusion, or the longings in our lives. We can be thankful, though, that we have a loving heavenly Father who stands ready to help.

The peace of God cannot be explained. It cannot be bought. The world cannot give it to us. But when we release our cares to the Lord in prayer, His peace washes over us and fills our hearts and minds. What a comfort is the peace of God when we find ourselves in the valley.

*Sovereign God, draw near to me and replace my
worry with Your peace. Amen.*

# Silence

*He was oppressed, and he was afflicted, yet he opened
not his mouth; like a lamb that is led to the slaughter,
and like a sheep that before its shearers
is silent, so he opened not his mouth.*

ISAIAH 53:7 ESV

Jesus' silence can teach us important lessons. Underneath
His silence was an implicit trust in His Father and His
purposes. Christ knew who He was and what He had
come to do.

Perhaps He was praying silently as He stood before
Pilate. It is often in the stillness of our lives that we hear
God best. When we take time to think, meditate on scripture, pray, and reflect, we find that we can indeed hear the
still, small voice. Many of us avoid quiet and solitude with
constant noise and busyness. But important things happen
in the silence. The Father can speak; we can listen. We can
speak, knowing He is listening. Trust is built in silence,
and confidence strengthens in silence.

*Lord Jesus, help me to learn from Your silence. Help me
to trust You more so that I don't feel the need to explain
myself. Give me the desire and the courage to be alone
with You and learn to hear Your voice. Amen.*

# Faith, the Emotional Balancer

*No man is justified by the law in the sight of God,
it is evident: for, The just shall live by faith.*
GALATIANS 3:11 KJV

Emotions mislead us. One day shines with promise as we bounce out of bed in song, while the next day dims in despair and we'd prefer to hide under the bedcovers. One moment we forgive, the next we harbor resentment.

The emotional roller coaster thrusts us into mood changes and affects what we do, what we say, and the attitudes that define us.

It has been said that faith is the bird that feels the light and sings to greet the dawn while it is still dark. The Bible instructs us to live by faith—not by feelings. Faith assures us that daylight will dawn in our darkest moments, affirming God's presence so that even when we fail to pray and positive feelings fade, our moods surrender to song.

*Heavenly Father, I desire for my faith, not my emotions,
to dictate my life. I pray for balance in my hide-
under-the-covers days, so that I might
surrender to You in song. Amen.*

# Follow the Lord's Footsteps

*"Come, follow me," Jesus said,
"and I will send you out to fish for people."*
MATTHEW 4:19 NIV

Jesus asked His disciples to follow Him, and He asks us to do the same. It sounds simple, but following Jesus can be a challenge. Sometimes we become impatient, not wanting to wait upon the Lord. We run ahead of Him by taking matters into our own hands and making decisions without consulting Him first. Or perhaps we aren't diligent to keep in step with Him. We fall behind, and soon Jesus seems so far away.

Following Jesus requires staying right on His heels. We need to be close enough to hear His whisper. Stay close to His heart by opening the Bible daily. Allow His Word to speak to your heart and give you direction. Throughout the day, offer up prayers for guidance and wisdom. Keep in step with Him, and His close presence will bless you beyond measure.

*Dear Lord, grant me the desire to follow You.
Help me not to run ahead or lag behind. Amen.*

# Truth in Love

*O LORD, I know the way of man is not in himself;*
*it is not in man who walks to direct his own steps.*
*O LORD, correct me, but with justice; not in*
*Your anger, lest You bring me to nothing.*
JEREMIAH 10:23–24 NKJV

Though confrontation is difficult, if we love someone, it is good and right to speak the truth in love. Jeremiah 17:9 tells us that our own hearts are wicked, and we can't understand our own feelings and actions. Our tendency is to rationalize our sinful behavior. Thankfully, God has given us the gift of the Holy Spirit to help us on our journey. If we ask, the Lord is faithful to His Word and He will reveal our motivations to us. We can use Jeremiah's words as our prayer, asking God to correct us, to show us what is true and how to live in light of it.

*Thank You, Father, that You are the discerner of hearts,*
*that You gently show me my sin, and that You have*
*given me Your Holy Spirit to help me. Amen.*

# A Different Cup to Fill

*O God, thou art my God;*
*early will I seek thee.*
PSALM 63:1 KJV

King David presided over the nation of Israel and all that that entailed. Yet he found time to seek the counsel, mercy, and direction of God daily. The more responsibilities he assumed, the more he prayed and meditated on God's precepts. Well before David was inundated with worldly concerns, nagging obligations, and his administrative duties, the Bible suggests that he sought the Lord in the early morning hours.

If the king of Israel recognized his need to spend time with God, how much more should we? When we seek our heavenly Father before daily activities demand our attention, the Holy Spirit regenerates our spirits, and our cups overflow.

*Dear Lord, I take this time to pray and spend time with You before I attend to daily responsibilities. Fill my cup with the presence and power of Your Spirit. Give me the wisdom and direction I need today. Amen.*

# Power Up

The Spirit of God, who raised Jesus
from the dead, lives in you.
ROMANS 8:11 NLT

It's natural to want to do things on our own. We all want to be independent and strong. When faced with a challenge, the first thing we do is try to work it out in our own skill and ability—within our own power. But there's another way.

We don't have to go it alone. Our heavenly Father wants to help. All we have to do is ask. He has already made His power available to His children. Whatever we face, wherever we go, whatever dreams we have for our lives, take courage and know that anything is possible when we draw on the power of God.

*Father, help me to remember that You are always with me, ready to help me do all things. Amen.*

## God's Mountain Sanctuary

*And seeing the multitudes, he went up into a
mountain. . .and. . .his disciples came unto him:
And he opened his mouth, and taught them.*
MATTHEW 5:1–2 KJV

Jesus often retreated to a mountain to pray. There He called
His disciples to depart from the multitudes so that He
could teach them valuable truths—the lessons we learn
from nature. Don't fret, obey God's gentle promptings,
and simply flow in the path He clears.

Do you yearn for a place where problems evaporate
like the morning dew? Do you need a place of solace?
God is wherever you are—behind a bedroom door, in your
favorite chair, or even at a sink full of dirty dishes. Come
apart and enter God's mountain sanctuary.

*Heavenly Father, I long to hear Your voice and to flow
in the path You clear before me. Help me to find
sanctuary in Your abiding presence. Amen.*

# Stand in the Gap

*"I looked for someone among them who would build up the*
*wall and stand before me in the gap on behalf of the land*
*so I would not have to destroy it, but I found no one."*
EZEKIEL 22:30 NIV

Each prayer request you offer up to God is important to
you, and when you ask others to pray, you're counting on
them to help carry you through the tough times.

It's easy in the busyness of life to overlook a request
someone else has made. Maybe you don't know the person
very well or you don't really have an understanding of what
he or she is going through. Perhaps the request came in
an e-mail that you quickly glanced at and then deleted.

Don't delay. Take time right when you receive a
request to talk to the Lord on the requester's behalf. Be
the bridge that carries that person through the valley of
darkness back to the mountaintop of joy.

*Heavenly Father, help me to have a heart of compassion*
*for those I know and even for those I don't know who*
*need Your comfort and love. Help me never to*
*be too busy to pray for them. Amen.*

## Perfect Prayers

*"Pray, then, in this way: Our Father. . ." Out of the depths [of distress] I have cried to You, O LORD.*
MATTHEW 6:9 AMP; PSALM 130:1 AMP

How many times have we made prayer a mere religious exercise, performed best by the "holy elite," rather than what it really is—conversation with God our Father?

Just pour out your heart to God. Share how your day went. Tell Him your dreams. Ask Him to search you and reveal areas of compromise. Thank Him for your lunch. Plead for your family and friends' well-being. Complain about your car. . . . Just talk with Him. Don't worry how impressive (or unimpressive!) you sound.

Talk with God while doing dishes, driving the car, folding laundry, eating lunch, or kneeling by your bed. Whenever, wherever, whatever—tell Him. He cares!

Don't allow this day to slip away without talking to your Father. No perfection required.

*Father God, what a privilege it is to unburden my heart to You. Teach me the beauty and simplicity of simply sharing my day with You. Amen.*

# Available 24-7

*I call on you, my God, for you will answer me;*
*turn your ear to me and hear my prayer.*
**PSALM 17:6 NIV**

We've all felt the frustration of that black hole called voice mail. It is rare to reach a real, honest-to-goodness, breathing human being the first time we dial a telephone number.

Fortunately, our God is always available. He can be reached at any hour of the day or night and every day of the year—including weekends and holidays! When we pray, we don't have to worry about disconnections, hang-ups, or poor reception. We will never be put on hold or our prayers diverted to another department. The Bible assures us that God is eager to hear our petitions and that He welcomes our prayers of thanksgiving. The psalmist David wrote of God's response to those who put their trust in Him: "He will call on me, and I will answer him" (Psalm 91:15 NIV). David had great confidence that God would hear his prayers. And we can too!

*Dear Lord, thank You for always being there for me.*
*Whether I am on a mountaintop and just want to*
*praise Your name or I am in need of Your comfort*
*and encouragement, I can count on You. Amen.*

# Anxiety Check!

*Do not be anxious about anything, but in every situation,*
*by prayer and petition, with thanksgiving,*
*present your requests to God.*
PHILIPPIANS 4:6 NIV

Twenty-first-century women are always checking things. A bank balance. Email. Voice messages. The grocery list. And, of course, that never-ending to-do list. We routinely get our oil, tires, and brake fluid checked. And we wouldn't think of leaving home for the day without checking our appearance in the mirror. We even double-check our purses, making sure we have the essentials—lipstick, mascara, and the cell phone.

When was the last time you did an anxiety check? Days? Weeks? Months? Chances are, you're due for another. After all, we're instructed not to be anxious about anything. Instead, we're to present our requests to God with thanksgiving in our hearts. We're to turn to Him in prayer so that He can take our burdens. Once they've lifted, it's bye-bye anxiety!

*Father, I get anxious sometimes. And I don't*
*always remember to turn to You with my anxiety.*
*In fact, I forget to check for anxiety at all.*
*Today I hand my anxieties to You. Amen.*

# Order in Our Prayers

*First of all, then, I urge that entreaties and prayers,
petitions and thanksgivings, be made on behalf of all men,
for kings and all who are in authority, so that we may
lead a tranquil and quiet life in all godliness and dignity.*
1 TIMOTHY 2:1–2 NASB

The demands of this world, and the pace at which our technology is racing, can sometimes overwhelm us, causing feelings of panic, powerlessness, and even paranoia. Is there a solution that brings life back into perspective? Yes. And God calls it prayer.

Our human sense of ineptness—we simply aren't equal to the task of being in charge of the universe—causes us to react to pressure. So, we've got to release the hand controls back to God. And when we practice this on an individual level, the prayers we offer within our congregations become more effective.

Prayer isn't some mystical activity to be attained by a few saintly little ladies in the church. Instead, it is an act of worship on the part of the created toward the Creator. Prayer is simply talking to God about everything that affects our lives.

*Spirit of God, fall afresh on me that I might
lift my voice in petition to You. Amen.*

# New Every Morning

*Because of the LORD's great love we are not consumed,
for his compassions never fail. They are new
every morning; great is your faithfulness.*
LAMENTATIONS 3:22–23 NIV

God starts out His day offering renewed compassion to His children. No matter what trials, difficulties, and sins yesterday brought, the morning ushers in a fresh experience, a brand-new beginning for believers who seek His forgiveness. All you have to do is accept the gift.

Are you burdened from yesterday's stress? Are the worries of tomorrow keeping you awake at night? Consider the dawning of the day as an opportunity to begin anew with our heavenly Father. Seek Him in the morning through studying His Word and through prayer, embracing His compassion to be a blessing to others throughout your day.

*Father, Your promise of never-ending compassion for me
is amazing! I never want to take for granted the grace
You offer every day. I'm so undeserving, but still You
give and give and give. Please help me to show mercy
to others the same way You do to me. Amen.*

# Run the Race

*Therefore, since we are surrounded by such a great cloud of witnesses, let us throw off everything that hinders and the sin that so easily entangles. And let us run with perseverance the race marked out for us.*
HEBREWS 12:1 NIV

A Christian's journey is much like a marathon. The road isn't always easy. Spiritual training is required to keep going and finish the race. Train by reading and obeying God's Word. Discipline yourself to keep your eyes on Jesus at all times. Be determined to spend time in prayer.

The writer of Hebrews reminds us that others are watching. Let their cheers bring encouragement. Let their presence inspire and motivate. Be quick to confess sin in order to run the race unhindered. Persevere. Jesus waits at the finish line. The reward will be well worth it!

*Dear Lord, help me run this Christian race with perseverance. Amen.*

# Learning as We Grow

*"But I am only a little child and do not know how to carry out my duties."*
1 KINGS 3:7 NIV

When King David died, Solomon became the king of Israel. Just like a child who does not yet know how to put away his toys, Solomon confesses that he does not know how to carry out his duties as king of Israel. Instead of sitting down on his throne in despair, though, Solomon calls on the name of the Lord for help.

As Christians, we are sometimes like little children. We know what our duties as Christians are, but we do not know how to carry them out. Just like Solomon, we can ask God for help and guidance in the completion of our responsibilities. God hears our prayers and is faithful in teaching us our duties, just as He was faithful to Solomon in teaching him his.

*Dear Lord, thank You for being willing to teach me my Christian responsibilities. Help me to learn willingly and eagerly. Amen.*

# Jonah's Prayer

*"In my distress I called to the LORD, and he answered me.*
*From deep in the realm of the dead I called for help,*
*and you listened to my cry."*
**JONAH 2:2 NIV**

Jonah's prayer is distinctive because he's praying from the belly of a large fish—a seemingly hopeless situation. The response you might expect is, "Lord, get me out of here!" Instead, Jonah praises God for listening to and answering him! He prays with gratitude and praise as well as with contrition.

Jonah's example is helpful to Christians today. He teaches us that even in our worst situations we need to approach God with both repentance and thanksgiving. No matter our experiences, we serve a powerful God—One who deserves all honor and praise.

*Dear Lord, thank You for hearing my prayers.*
*Thank You for having mercy on me. Amen.*

# A Faithful Example

*"Surely your God is a God of gods and a Lord of kings
and a revealer of mysteries, since you have
been able to reveal this mystery."*

**DANIEL 2:47 NASB**

Maybe you have a friend, coworker, or family member who has not yet put his or her faith in God. Perhaps you have been praying about it for many years. Don't give up hope! Daniel's faith allowed God to demonstrate His power to the king, and while the king did not immediately bow down to God, he saw that God was real and powerful.

Our faithful example is important. When we trust in God, those around us will see His power in us. Through our actions, others will come to know God and proclaim that He is a God of gods and a Lord of kings.

*Dear Lord, be with my friends who don't know You.
Help me to plant seeds of faith in their hearts.
Let me trust that You will make them grow. Amen.*

# Christ Is Involved

*Being confident of this very thing, that he which
hath begun a good work in you will perform
it until the day of Jesus Christ.*
**PHILIPPIANS 1:6 KJV**

Christ wants you to grow in your faith. He wants to help
you flee the temptations that you will inevitably face.
He wants to give you strength to be joyful even as you go
through trials. His ultimate desire is to help you become
more like Him.

Do you allow Jesus to be as involved in your life as He
wants to be? Unfortunately, a lot of people accept Him in
order to get into heaven, but then they want little more to
do with Him. Why not choose now to let Him be a part
of everything you do and every decision you make? Go
to Him in prayer. Seek answers from His Word and from
the Holy Spirit. He will do a great work in your life. He
will be faithful to complete what He started in you—and
you will become like Him.

*Dear Jesus, thank You for wanting to help me be like
You. Thank You for being involved in my life and
not leaving me to my own designs. Amen.*

# Loyalty to Family

*Then Orpah kissed her mother-in-law
goodbye, but Ruth clung to her.*
RUTH 1:14 NIV

Orpah went back to her homeland, but Ruth remained with her mother-in-law. Naomi urged her to leave, but Ruth wouldn't go.

Ruth refused to worry about the future or to look out only for her own good. She put a high priority on the welfare of her mother-in-law. She stood by her in her time of need.

Do you have a family member who needs your loyalty? Maybe it is your spouse, a parent, child, sibling, or an in-law. Perhaps there is someone in your family who has been a blessing to you and whom you can bless in return. Or maybe you have a relative who has let everyone down, someone who truly does not even deserve your faithfulness—but who desperately needs it. Pray that God will show you the Naomi in your life. He will honor your faithfulness to family.

*Father, help me to be faithful to my family. Amen.*

# Freedom

*Exercise your freedom by serving God, not by breaking the rules. Treat everyone you meet with dignity. Love your spiritual family. Revere God. Respect the government.*
1 PETER 2:16–17 MSG

Paul tells us in 1 Corinthians 10:23 (NIV) that "'I have the right to do anything,' you say—but not everything is beneficial. 'I have the right to do anything'—but not everything is constructive." We must be careful and responsible with our freedom. Paul warns us not to cause anyone to stumble, and that everything we do should be done to the glory of God.

Are you a responsible Christian? Is there anything in your life that is causing someone in your life to stumble? Could it be the television shows you watch, the types of movies you frequent, or maybe even your spending habits? Take this to the Lord in prayer and ask Him to search your heart and show you anything that may be hindering another person in her walk with Christ.

*Father, help me to be responsible with my freedom. Please help me to change anything in my life that might be causing someone else to stumble. Amen.*

# Attention and Prayer

*Pray in the Spirit at all times and on every occasion.*
*Stay alert and be persistent in your prayers*
*for all believers everywhere.*
EPHESIANS 6:18 NLT

Paul must have known how difficult prayer could be. He realized the kind of prayer he describes in Ephesians is demanding, but he also knew that it is the most fulfilling and valuable type of prayer. Paul encourages us to work hard at prayer, being constant, alert, and attending to Christians everywhere.

Persistence and consistency are difficult, but Paul's most challenging instruction is to pray for all Christians everywhere. In today's society, getting wrapped up in our own lives is too easy. Even when we look outside ourselves, we often limit prayer to family and friends, or at most, our local church family. We must look further. Praying for Christians everywhere requires us to engage in a world we might not always be involved with, but God wants us to pray for our Christian family whether they are around the corner or around the world.

*Dear Lord, help me to be consistent in my prayers,*
*and to remember to pray for my Christian*
*family throughout the world. Amen.*

# *Praying for Loved Ones*

> *"Therefore I tell you, whatever you ask for in prayer,*
> *believe that you have received it, and it will be yours."*
> MARK 11:24 NIV

One of the best things a woman can do for her loved ones is pray for them. And while we don't find one simple formula for effective prayer in the Bible, *how* we pray may be just as important as *what* we pray.

Do we beseech God with faith, believing that He can do anything? Or do we pray with hesitation, believing that nothing is going to change? God is honored and willing to work when we pray with faith.

The most beneficial times of prayer often come when we make time to listen to God, not just talk "at" Him. He can give us wisdom and insights we would never come up with on our own.

Though we can't always see it, He is at work, in our loved ones' hearts and in ours.

*Lord, thank You for Your concern for my friends*
*and family members. I know You love them*
*even more than I do. Amen.*

# Prayers for Boldness

*Pray that I may declare [the gospel] fearlessly, as I should.*
EPHESIANS 6:20 NIV

In Ephesians 6:20, Paul asks the Ephesians to pray for him. He realized that without the prayers of the saints and the faithfulness of God, he would not be an effective ambassador for Christ.

In today's world, proclaiming our faith can be difficult. Our family, friends, and coworkers can make us feel shy about sharing the Gospel. We might feel unworthy to talk about our faith, or we may be worried that we will not use the right words. Paul's request for prayer should encourage us. Paul, too, worried about his ability to effectively communicate the Gospel to those around him. He relied on his brothers and sisters in Christ to lift him up to God. In the same way, we should rely on our brothers and sisters to pray for us, that we may declare the Gospel fearlessly, as we should.

*Dear Lord, thank You for Your Word. Surround me with people who will pray for me, and place people in my life for whom I can pray. Together let us boldly proclaim Your name. Amen.*

# Peace Is a Guard

*Do not be anxious about anything, but in every situation,
by prayer and petition, with thanksgiving, present your
requests to God. And the peace of God, which transcends
all understanding, will guard your hearts
and your minds in Christ Jesus.*

PHILIPPIANS 4:6–7 NIV

Worry will try to attack us on a regular basis. Fear can so
easily creep into our thinking and rob us of joy, the very
treasure we hold because we know Christ.

Thankfully, we have been given the key to protecting
our minds and hearts—prayer. In coming to God with
our petitions and in giving thanks to Him for all He has
already done for us, we receive His peace. Beyond our
ability to understand or explain, a heaven-sent peace
will abide with us.

What a beautiful picture: the soldier of peace standing
at the door of our hearts and minds, guarding the treasure
of fellowship with Christ. It is ours for the asking when
we go to our Father with all our requests.

*Father, cause me to remember that Your peace is available
to guard me night and day. Help me to bring everything to
You in prayer, trusting in Your faithful provision. Amen.*

# A Woman Who Fears the Lord

*Charm is deceptive, and beauty is fleeting; but a woman who fears the LORD is to be praised. Honor her for all that her hands have done, and let her works bring her praise at the city gate.*
**PROVERBS 31:30–31 NIV**

Charm and beauty are not the attributes that God values in His daughters. Clearly, it is a healthy and holy respect for the Father that sets apart believers from the lost. Through Bible study and prayer, we get to know God better. In the Old Testament, He is a God of order, a jealous God. In the New Testament, He is consistent and faithful, offering up His great sacrifice in His Son, Jesus.

Ask the Lord to help you develop a true reverence for Him. He wants us to call Him *Abba* Father ("Daddy"), but He also demands respect, reverence, and a holy fear. He is the God of the universe—the same yesterday, today, and tomorrow.

*God, make me a woman who respects You deeply, I pray. Amen.*

# Soul-Cravings

*As the deer pants for streams of water, so my soul pants
for you, my God. My soul thirsts for God, for the living
God. When can I go and meet with God?*

PSALM 42:1–2 NIV

Our hearts have some indefinable yearnings. We look for
fulfillment from people, titles, achievement, chocolate. We
may attempt to squelch the longings with distractions of
busyness, fashion, an extra drink, motherhood, or even
church work. But the longing is a thirst for intimate connection with our God. Our souls pant for Him! He alone
quenches our needs.

The Spirit knows our subtle moods, our hearts' aches,
and our soul-cravings. We must turn to Him in transparent
prayer, mulling the Word over in our minds, allowing it to
penetrate the hidden recesses of our souls.

*God, You are the headwaters of life for me. Reveal the
substitutes I look to for fulfillment. Help me to drink
deeply from Your Word and Your abiding Spirit,
that I might be complete in You. Amen.*

# Prayer Reveals Our Dependence

*Then Jesus went with his disciples to a place
called Gethsemane, and he said to them,
"Sit here while I go over there and pray."*
MATTHEW 26:36 NIV

Jesus was humble. He conceded that He needed help.
He admitted His human weakness. He acknowledged
His struggle in the Garden of Gethsemane. Confiding
in His disciples, He revealed His anguish and pain. Then
He turned to His heavenly Father. Jesus knew He needed
God's help to endure the cross. Prayer revealed Jesus' utter
dependence on God.

How much do you really need God? Your prayer life
reveals your answer. If an independent attitude has crept
into it, prayer may seem a ritualistic exercise. But if you
realize your weakness and acknowledge your need, then
prayer will become vital to your existence. It will become
your sustenance and nourishment—your lifeline. Prayer
reveals your dependence upon God. How much do you
need Him?

*Dear Lord, I truly need You. May my prayer life
demonstrate my dependence upon You. Amen.*

# The Blues

---

*Why, my soul, are you downcast? Why so disturbed within me? Put your hope in God, for I will yet praise him, my Savior and my God.*

PSALM 42:11 NIV

Has your soul ever felt weighed down? Everyone experiences times when frustrations seem to outweigh joy, but as Christians, we have an unending source of encouragement in God.

*That's great,* you may think, *but how am I supposed to tap into that joy?* First, pray. Ask God to unburden your spirit. Share your stress, frustrations, and worries with Him. Don't hold back; He can take it. Make a list of the blessings in your life and thank the Provider of those blessings. Choose to not focus on yourself; instead, praise Him for being Him.

Soon you'll feel true, holy refreshment—the freedom God wants you to live out every day.

*Rejuvenate my spirit, Lord! You alone can take away the burden I feel. You are my hope and my redeemer forever. Amen.*

# Faithfulness and Obedience

*"O LORD, God of Israel, there is no God like you
in all of heaven and earth. You keep your covenant
and show unfailing love to all who walk before
you in wholehearted devotion."*

2 CHRONICLES 6:14 NLT

After seven years of hard work, thousands of workmen, and unfathomable amounts of money, Solomon finally completed the temple. The priests carried the ark of the Lord's covenant into the inner room of the sanctuary, and suddenly, the presence of God appeared in the form of a cloud. The people were overjoyed, and Solomon led them in this prayer of thanksgiving and praise.

Sometimes, as God's people, we can be overwhelmed by the requests God makes of us. We may not be expected to build a temple, but God certainly asks us to obey Him in other ways. Thankfully, when we feel overcome with panic, we can rely on God's loving faithfulness to see us through our challenges. We simply must acknowledge God's power and eagerly obey His will.

*Dear Lord, truly You are the one true God in all creation.
Thank You for Your faithfulness and unfailing love.
Teach me to eagerly obey Your will. Amen.*

## Skinnier Times

*Keep your lives free from the love of money and be content with what you have, because God has said, "Never will I leave you; never will I forsake you."*

HEBREWS 13:5 NIV

It can seem like God has left, when you are bone-weary, working for meager earnings, giving all you've got, and the creditors are banging at the doors of your deficit account. You ask, "Where are you, God?"

Life's richest lessons come from our hard times. It is *there* that we are stripped of our self-sufficiency. We can see life from a perspective we miss in cushy-comfort times when we feel less of a need to come to God in prayer. When we have need, we cry out to Him. In those times, He becomes our sufficiency, and we learn His resources are inexhaustible. His presence and comfort are irreplaceable. These lessons from skinnier times deepen our walk with Christ, bringing more contentment for what we have.

*God, You've promised to never leave or forsake me. Help me to remember that in the sparse times You are there with me. I can be content because it all flows from Your hand. Amen.*

# Remember

―――――❦―――――

*"I am the LORD your God, who brought you
out of Egypt, out of the land of slavery."*
EXODUS 20:2 NIV

Just before God gave the Israelites the Ten Command-
ments, He reminded them that He had brought them out
of slavery in Egypt. It is easy for us to read this verse and
wonder why the Israelites needed reminding. After years
and years of harsh treatment and manual labor in Egypt,
wouldn't they always be grateful to the Lord for delivering
them from slavery?

Establish some reminders of God's blessings. Start a
prayer journal where you can record your prayer requests
and God's answers. Review the pages of your prayer journal
when you face a hardship. Thank God for taking care of you
in the past and ask Him to increase your faith. He wants
you to trust that He will never leave you or forsake you.

Like the Israelites, we forget. God is faithful in *all
ways* for *all days*. Remember that today.

*You are faithful, Father. You have freed me from
the gates of hell and given me an abundant life with
the promise of eternity with You. Grow my
faith. Help me to remember. Amen.*

# Skeptics and Cynics

*For ever since the world was created, people have seen*
*the earth and sky. Through everything God made,*
*they can clearly see his invisible qualities—*
*his eternal power and divine nature.*
*So they have no excuse for not knowing God.*
ROMANS 1:20 NLT

There are skeptics and cynics in our world. They love to question the possibility of a divine Creator. They have seemingly sound arguments based in logic and science. We can share testimonials, blessings, and miracles from our personal lives and from scripture. But these are often met with disbelief and tales of big bangs and evolution.

In order for a skeptic to be changed to a seeker, Jesus must grab his attention, often using His children to do that. Take time to really consider the miraculous works of God that prove His existence. Pray for wisdom and compelling words to lead cynics to the throne.

*Father, help me to be a good witness of You and Your*
*miraculous wonders. Give me the words to convince even*
*the most hardened skeptic. Guide me to people, according*
*to Your will, so that I can make a difference. Amen.*

# The Nearness of You

*Come near to God and he will come near to you.*
JAMES 4:8 NIV

"Come near to God," we hear. And we think, *I can do that.* So we take our notebooks and buy the most inspirational Bibles complete with ribbon bookmarks and study notes, we create quiet-time nooks, we go sit under trees, we spiritually retreat and. . .find we are no closer. We don't feel closer to God; we feel tired.

So we follow the rest of James' instructions. We pray, we pour our hearts out, and maybe even cry. We humbly admit our faults to God. Finally, James says, "*Now* you've got it!" Because it was never about us making ourselves any better. We are messed-up people. Even our best efforts at doing better are going to get us nowhere in the end. Once we humbly admit that fact, God will lift us up. And *that's* how we get nearer, by realizing we can't do anything without Him.

*My God, my Friend, my Lover, my Savior.*
*Humble me, so You can lift me up. Amen.*

## All Too Familiar

*"God, I thank you that I am not like other people."*
LUKE 18:11 NIV

Have you ever said this prayer? Or one like it? "Thank God, we aren't that bad." "Good heavens, I'm glad no one I know is like that!" "Well, we might not be perfect, but at least we've never _____!" (Fill in the blank with an appropriate sin.)

Perhaps you've never said such words, or even thought them, but could it be that you have, somewhere in a small corner of your mind, felt just a little bit better than other people? A little more worthy? A little more deserving?

Jesus sets us straight. It was the other guy who "went home justified" (Luke 18:14). The tax collector. The guy who wouldn't even look up. The guy who stood at a distance, beating the words out of his chest, "Have mercy on me, a sinner" (Luke 18:13). The two prayers could not have been more different. The two pray-ers? They had a lot in common.

*God, if I ever start thinking of myself as better than someone else, show me the truth. Amen.*

# Family Picture

*How wonderful, how beautiful,
when brothers and sisters get along!*
PSALM 133:1 MSG

What do you think the church's family picture would look like? If we could somehow manage to get all the people in all the congregations around the world to sit still and look nice for just ten seconds, what would happen? Would the photo be all lovely and Olan Mills perfect? Or would it show fingers pointing in accusation, someone getting knocked over, someone's feelings getting hurt, tears, bruises. . .anarchy?

It's highly unlikely we can do much about the world's Christian population in general, but what can we do in our own communities to make a better family photo? What can we do to become a better family?

Pray to promote peace, love, and unity between our brothers and sisters, beginning with ourselves.

*Dear God, let me be an instrument of Your peace.
Help me, in whatever conversations or relationships
I develop, to build up unity among Your followers. Amen.*

# Grief-Worn

*Heal me, LORD, for my bones are in agony. My soul is
in deep anguish. How long, LORD, how long?*
PSALM 6:2–3 NIV

We struggle to find ways of expressing the bone-crushing
weariness of grief. Sometimes it feels as though if we could
just put it into words, maybe we could get past the sorrow.

But the psalmists have given us words: "I am worn
out from my groaning. All night long I flood my bed with
weeping and drench my couch with tears. My eyes grow
weak with sorrow; they fail because of all my foes" (vv. 6–7).

It is somehow comforting to know that souls from
thousands of years ago can speak to us about the same
feelings we have today. And that even though there is
still pain and trouble and sorrow, there is also still our
Lord God, who never changes: "The LORD has heard my
weeping. The LORD has heard my cry for mercy; the LORD
accepts my prayer" (vv. 8–9).

*Dear God, hear me when I am sad and feel alone.
Show me You are with me, and that my grief
will not go on forever. Amen.*

# Whatever You Ask

*"If you believe, you will receive whatever you ask for in prayer."*
MATTHEW 21:22 NIV

The sky's the limit. That's essentially what Jesus told His disciples here. He said you can make a fig tree wither with a word, or have a mountain throw itself into the sea. Magical things. The stuff of fairy tales.

Do you really believe? Will you receive whatever you ask?

Christians have nice answers for these questions when younger Christians ask them. We say that God works through our prayers; that if we are in God's will, that we will ask for things that God wants to happen anyway. That if we don't have the right motives, we won't get what we ask.

And those things are all most likely true. But this illustration Jesus made here to His disciples has a different flavor to it, doesn't it? Here He seems to be pushing us to want something more. Something we think is impossible.

So what is your mountain?

*God, help me truly believe. Amen.*

# Enforced Gratitude

*They were also to stand every morning
to thank and praise the LORD.*

1 CHRONICLES 23:30 NIV

David appointed the Levites to help Aaron's descendants with the service of the temple of the Lord. One of their jobs was to "stand every morning to thank and praise the LORD." They did this in the evening as well.

They also had thank offerings. It seems it would be far easier at times to offer a thank offering to burn—would handmade sweaters work?—than to actually say words of thanks, and far, far simpler than actually feeling thankful.

But for every awkward gift we receive, or uncomfortable moment in life we endure, there must be at least a hundred good things our Father gives us that we can and should feel thankful for.

So try it. . . Appoint yourself to be your own Levite. Get up and stand every morning and thank and praise the Lord!

*Dear Lord, I give thanks to You, for You are good,
and Your love endures forever. Amen.*

# *Even If He Doesn't*

*"The God we serve is able to deliver us."*
DANIEL 3:17 NIV

Shadrach, Meshach, and Abednego, followers of the one true God, refused to worship Nebuchadnezzar's idol. They knew what would happen to them for disobeying the king's orders, and they still refused, saying, "If we are thrown into the blazing furnace, the God we serve is able to deliver us from it, and he will deliver us from Your Majesty's hand" (Daniel 3:17 NIV). They definitely had confidence in their God.

But that wasn't all they said: "But even if he does not, we want you to know, Your Majesty, that we will not serve your gods or worship the image of gold you have set up" (v. 18). "Even if he does not."

Have you been praying hard for something to happen recently? Something you really care about? Are you able to pray those words too: "God, even if you do not. . ."?

*Help me, Lord, to believe even*
*when things don't go my way. Amen.*

## God Knows

*"Do not be like them, for your Father knows what you need before you ask him."*
MATTHEW 6:8 NIV

"Them" in Matthew 6:8 are an interesting crew. Jesus describes them in verse 7, saying: "When you pray, do not keep on babbling like pagans, for they think they will be heard because of their many words." Jesus is telling the believers not to be babblers. It sounds like people were having trouble figuring out prayer even back then.

Jesus wants us to be less concerned with our style of prayer and more concerned with what we say, and who we are saying it to.

The pagans go on babbling perhaps because they can't be quite certain who it is they are talking to, or what it is they want their god(s) to do. But we have a Father in heaven who is holy and in control. We know who He is, and He knows us. And we do not have to use many words to make our needs known.

We do not pray to offer God information. We pray to offer God us.

*Dear God, thank You for hearing my imperfect prayers. Amen.*

# *The Grass Is Always Greener*

*And the peace of God, which transcends all understanding,*
*will guard your hearts and your minds in Christ Jesus.*
PHILIPPIANS 4:7 NIV

When staring at everyone else's journey, you're bound to stumble on the road. Many times other people's lives appear happier, richer, fuller, maybe even more sanctified by God. When envy settles in, you tend to lose your grateful heart. You lose your way. And Satan is right there escorting you off the path and into a journey you were never meant to take—a fearsome passage you were never meant to walk. One without joy, laughter, hope, or—peace.

Comparisons can mean a slow death of the spirit. The moment you catch yourself with the-grass-is-always-greener mentality, know that it will only lead you astray. So, stay prayerfully focused on God and His way for you. Then the peace that passes all understanding will not be a distant mirage, but authentic, and yours.

*God, help me to be content and at peace with myself*
*and the life You have given me. I am unique*
*and valuable in Your eyes. Amen.*

# Do Not Be Discouraged

*"I have told you these things, so that in me you may
have peace. In this world you will have trouble.
But take heart! I have overcome the world."*

JOHN 16:33 NIV

Perhaps your prayer life feels a little like gazing out at the
calm surface of the sea, but all the while you're thinking
that your mighty supplications should be building and
frothing those waves up into a real storm of answered
prayers. But even when the sea seems quiet—as if nothing
is happening—the oceans are shifting and traveling all
around the world. God is also moving, sometimes just
below the surface where we can't perceive it, but He is
ever working things for good.

Remember, God wants His children to have peace
and hope. The Lord declares in His Word that He has
plans to prosper you and not to harm you, plans to give
you hope and a future (Jeremiah 29:11). The Lord also
said, "In this world you will have trouble. But take heart!
I have overcome the world."

Accept His comfort. Live His commands. Embrace
His love.

*God, help me to be persistent in prayer even when
I can't see the direct fruits of it. Amen.*

# One Word That Changes Everything

*He was despised and rejected by mankind, a man of
suffering, and familiar with pain. Like one from
whom people hide their faces he was despised,
and we held him in low esteem.*

**ISAIAH 53:3 NIV**

Have you ever felt abandoned? Misplaced? Abused? Rejected? Forgotten? We have all felt those feelings from time to time. What can we do about them? Well, the world has plenty of answers. Mask the anguish with painkillers, addictions, false teachings under the guise of spiritual enlightenment, and myriad other bogus remedies. You name it; the world is selling it as an alternative.

What to do? Face the unhappy pangs of this life by holding the hand of the One who has known all these trials—the One who knows better than anyone on earth what it feels like to suffer, to be rejected, abused, and forgotten. So, how does one do that, exactly? With the one word that the Enemy of our souls wants us to forget. One word that can change everything—can bring meaning and hope, and make that misery and aloneness flee to hell where it belongs: it's *prayer*.

*Father, help me to turn to You alone for
my comfort instead of to the world. Amen.*

# Tumbling the Stones

*But just as he who called you is holy,*
*so be holy in all you do.*
1 Peter 1:15–16 NIV

If you've ever spent time beachcombing, you know that the stones that get trapped in between the big rocks often get tossed and whirled a great deal. So much so, that the edges get worked off, making them the smoothest of all. The colors and nuances and unique markings are accentuated.

God uses the tumbling turbulence of our lives to work off our edges—those jagged, sinful, rebellious edges that keep us from being all that we were meant to be.

Being tumbled can be painful—stone hitting stone can't be all that fun—but the outcome will be holiness and a loveliness of spirit. We will be treasures, brighter than diamonds and more precious than gold.

Pray that God can use your tumbling trials to bring out the beauty of your soul.

*Dear Lord, please use the turbulent times of my life*
*to help make me beautiful in my spirit so that I can*
*glorify You and be all that You created me to be. Amen.*

# The Radiance of His Splendor

*In the year that King Uzziah died, I saw the Lord,*
*high and exalted, seated on a throne; and the train of his*
*robe filled the temple. Above him were seraphim, each with*
*six wings: With two wings they covered their faces, with*
*two they covered their feet, and with two they were flying.*
ISAIAH 6:1–2 NIV

The book of Isaiah tells us that the Lord is exalted, seated on a throne, and the train of His robe fills the temple. Isaiah also talks about the angels who attend Him and worship Him—that their wings cover their faces—surely because of the radiance of His splendor. How fearsome and humbling and magnificent that sight must be!

In fact, this holy scene in the heavens should remind us that one day every knee shall bow and every tongue confess that He is Lord. Why wait until that final day? Why not give praise to the One—the only One—who is worthy of our raised hearts and hands? The One who is truly incredible and awesome and glorious!

*Lord God, help me to comprehend Your magnitude*
*and glory. I want to be awestruck by You. Amen.*

# *The Most Beautiful Words*

*So God created mankind in his own image, in the image of God he created them; male and female he created them.*

GENESIS 1:27 NIV

We were made in the image of God, but because of sin, we became shriveled and faded. Yet with the sacrifice Jesus made for us with His very life, mankind has hope to return to the beauty that once was ours. When those who belong to Christ die and pass into eternity they will be given glorified bodies renewed with life and color. Not for a short time like the flowers of the field, but for all eternity.

If you've never asked the Lord to be yours, never acknowledged your sin and taken Him into your heart—well, what has been stopping you? They will be the most beautiful words you will ever speak and the most life-changing prayer you will ever pray.

*God, restore, refresh, and reconcile me to Yourself. Help me to become all You have created me to be. Amen.*

# That Volatile Liquid

*"Do not worry about your life, what you will eat or drink; or about your body, what you will wear. . . . Look at the birds of the air; they do not sow or reap or store away in barns, and yet your heavenly Father feeds them. Are you not much more valuable than they?"*
MATTHEW 6:25–26 NIV

Women tend to be like vats of worry. We toss everything imaginable into that emotional, messy brew. You know what I mean—the many frets that we distill down when we choose to hand-wring through our days and toss and turn through our nights. Then we pour that volatile liquid into spray bottles, and we hose down our friends and family with it.

Jesus asks us if we can add a single hour to our life with worry. We cannot. Jesus also says that the birds are cared for, and that we are much more valuable to Him than they are. So, what are we to do?

We can pray.

It's real. It's powerful. And our friends and family will thank us!

*Father, remind me that You're in control. I place my burdens and fears in Your capable hands. Amen.*

# When Life Hands You Lemons

*And we know that in all things God works for
the good of those who love him, who have
been called according to his purpose.*
**ROMANS 8:28 NIV**

You've heard the old saying that one should make lemonade out of the lemons that life hands you, and yet you wonder, "Where is the sugar? The chipped ice? The crystal pitcher to put it all in?"

And then you realize that the world expects you to provide all the extras with your own personal ingenuity and grit. Yet the steam that comes from our own strength will soon run out. We humans weren't meant to go it alone. We were meant for a relationship with God. Through Christ, that sweet connection is restored. He is the One who will help us. He promises us that if we love Him, He will work all things for good. He will redeem all things. He alone has the power to make the sweetest lemonade out of the sourest of lemons. What a promise. What a prayer!

*Father, thank You for taking what is miserable
and tragic and working it for good through Your power
and sovereignty. Help me to trust in Your promises. Amen.*

## The Voice of Heaven

*Jesus answered, "I am the way and the truth and the life.
No one comes to the Father except through me."*
John 14:6 NIV

The world never seems to be in sync with what God wants for us, dreams for us. We get the idea that what the fallen earth has to offer is more fascinating and glorious and irresistible. Yet how can that be, when people fail us and everything that *can* fall apart *does* fall apart? When even the kings and queens of this earth are destined to the same lonely and hopeless end without divine assistance?

There are no answers in this earthy dust, only in the voice of heaven. We should look up to our hope—for it lies in Christ and Christ alone. He is life, not death. He is the most fascinating and glorious and irresistible hope there ever was or ever will be. This could be our heart-praise as dawn arrives and as the sun sets.

*God, You are the answer to the riddles and the problems
of life. You are the salve for my sin-sick soul. Amen.*

# Do You Believe in Miracles?

*Now while he was in Jerusalem at the Passover*
*Festival, many people saw the signs he was*
*performing and believed in his name.*
JOHN 2:23 NIV

Jesus asks us to believe in miracles. Do you?

God does answer every prayer. It just may not fit
our agenda. And. . .when miracles do come, it is easy to
forget as the Israelites did, even though they witnessed
miracle after miracle after miracle. Still, they doubted.

That is the nature of man.

So let us keep a prayer journal and write down the
answers to our prayers, the miracles we experience. They
do happen. The journal will be a reminder that God is listening. That God does care about our comings and goings.
That He is still all-powerful and able to perform signs and
wonders. When the miracles do come, write them down.
Praise Him for them. Tell others. From time to time, we
should go back and read the journal, see the long list of
His tender mercies, so that we might be encouraged.

What miracle are you praying for today?

*Lord, don't let me forget the countless prayers You have*
*answered. Don't let me doubt the power of prayer. Amen.*

# All of the Above

*For the LORD gives wisdom; from his mouth come knowledge and understanding.*

**PROVERBS 2:6 NIV**

It's so easy to fall into the trap of thinking that if we simply pray about an issue, God will give us the answer—and in fairly short order. Because God knows we need all the answers we need when we need them, and not a moment later. Right?

It seems that often when we want an answer, the only thing that will do is the answer we want. Nothing less. Yet God, our generous Father, has something better in mind. We want a solution; He wants to give us the formula. We want a simple yes or no; He wants to give us time to see if we even asked the right question. We want A, B, C, or D; He wants to give us all of the above.

*Thank You, Lord, that Your ways are higher and wiser and better than mine. Help me to be patient when I lack wisdom, and to seek Your knowledge and understanding. Amen.*

# A Source of Comfort

*Praise be to the God and Father of our Lord Jesus Christ,*
*the Father of compassion and the God of all comfort,*
*who comforts us in all our troubles, so that we*
*can comfort those in any trouble.*
2 CORINTHIANS 1:3–4 NIV

Everyone has their favorite sources of comfort. When a work day hasn't gone well, or a rather large bill has arrived, a fight has occurred, or a loved one is suffering, people reach out for a security blanket—in the form of a person, place, or thing. Humans need a tangible reminder of safety, peace, and strength.

God loves us so much, He feels our worries and bears our troubles, and reaches out to us through His words and His songs and His reminders of love that come in all the little ways He knows will suit us best. He comforts us through the hands and feet of others who embrace us and walk beside us in hard times.

*Lord, help me to be a comfort to others*
*in the ways You comfort me. Amen.*

# Commanding Presence

*Trouble and distress have come upon me,*
*but your commands give me delight.*
PSALM 119:143 NIV

The word *commands* is not generally seen in a positive light.

Yet God commands. When people come into His commanding presence in prayer, they do find comfort. Why? Because when the foundations of your life are shaken, you want to hold on to something that is real, that is true, that will not and cannot be moved. The law of the Lord is that. Moreover, His law is *good*.

The more you meditate on His Word, the more you'll be convinced of this. Use the laws of God in your prayer time, and you will be forced to think about others, to consider what it means to really live in community, and to put others before yourself. In that process, the sorrow and trouble that are weighing you down will not disappear but will be put in proper perspective, and thus, become a little bit of a lighter load.

*Lord, thank You for the comfort*
*You bring us in Your law. Amen.*

## Like a Tree

*Blessed is the one. . .whose delight is in the law of the*
*LORD, and who meditates on his law day and night.*
**PSALM 1:1–2 NIV**

A tree has no choice about where it is rooted. Through
a turn in the wind or the whim of a bird or the thought
of a gardener, a seed is planted in the ground. Then year
after year the tree grows there (or doesn't). The tree cannot
go for a walk or visit other grounds. So a tree planted by
streams of water is blessed indeed. That tree gets the benefit
of life-giving liquid along with the changing scenery the
stream brings under its boughs each day.

So a person who delights in God's Word is blessed by
it. It gives life, and it brings an unending array of characters
and circumstances to your mind, without you ever having
to take a step. You can stand strong in the knowledge of
God's commands and still experience a wealth of opportunities—and prosper!

*Dear Lord, Thank You for Your Word. Amen.*

# Not Your Battle

*"All those gathered here will know that it is not by sword or spear that the LORD saves; for the battle is the LORD's, and he will give all of you into our hands."*

1 SAMUEL 17:47 NIV

David was in an ugly fight. Goliath was not exactly a humble opponent. He was big and loud and mean and scary. The Israelites were not showing themselves to be especially brave at the time. So David, the shepherd, stepped into the middle of this mess armed not with swords and catapults and spears, and not even with a sling and a stone. No, David was armed with the strength and power and might of the living God.

You are too. Perhaps you haven't seen God rescue you from the paw of a lion or bear, as David had. Yet you can be confident that God is more than able to get you through whatever challenge you are facing. Spend some time with Him. Ask Him to help you. Place your battle in His capable hands.

*Dear Lord, please let me lean on You. Amen.*

# A Prayer to Arms

*Finally, be strong in the Lord and in his mighty power.*
EPHESIANS 6:10 NIV

Dear God, make my tongue speak Your truth. Wrap your Word around me tight like a belt—help it to hold all things together. Please mold for me a guard around my heart so that I can long to follow Your righteous path, and not the desires of this world.

Make me ready, Lord, with answers to those who ask questions and wonder about You. Help me not be afraid to speak, but to be confident in my replies because I know You are behind every word of the gospel of peace.

Make me strong so I can bear Your shield of faith, repelling insecurities and fears and doubts that are the weapons of my enemy. God, You know the words and thoughts and actions that sting me the most. Please help me let Your peace and the certainty of You be a salve on my soul.

*Fill my head and heart with Your Spirit so I can go out and bless others with the security of salvation in You. Amen.*

# Watching from the Reeds

*Then she placed the child in it and put it among the reeds along the bank of the Nile.*
EXODUS 2:3 NIV

There is very little emotion captured in the story of baby Moses. A woman has a baby. She can't hide him from the cruel government, which legislated his death, so she puts him in a basket in the river. No tears. No sound. The end.

It wasn't the end, thankfully, for baby Moses. It's hard to imagine that was the end for his mother either. Even after her daughter followed the baby boy, watching him be rescued by royalty; even after she finished nursing her son and gave him back to be raised by his adoptive family; even after the boy had grown up and fled the land—it seems likely that it wasn't the end of the story for Moses' mother.

How many mothers are there out there who have watched from the reeds and prayed? Say a prayer today for those mothers watching from the reeds.

*Dear Lord, thank You for the gift of life.*
*Please bless all those mothers who have made*
*sacrifices so their babies could survive. Amen.*

# Bargain

*It is better not to make a vow than
to make one and not fulfill it.*
ECCLESIASTES 5:5 NIV

God would be the worst person ever to bargain with. Why? He doesn't need anything. When you are trying to strike a deal, it's best to know what your counterpart needs—what they lack that you can offer.

The God who made time, who spun the earth into motion and placed the stars in the sky, does not need you. He does not need anything you have to offer. He does not need your promises. Especially the empty ones.

He does want you to come to Him. He does want to be near you. He does want to love you. He will give you everything you could ever need. Come near to God and He will come near to you. Not to negotiate a deal, but just to know Him more.

*Dear Father, if You'll love me,
I will have everything I need. Amen.*

## Helper of the Fatherless

*But you, God, see the trouble of the afflicted; you consider*
*their grief and take it in hand. The victims commit*
*themselves to you; you are the helper of the fatherless.*
PSALM 10:14 NIV

Losing a parent shakes a person's foundations. Both sons
and daughters feel this loss keenly, though perhaps some-
what differently. For sons, it is the loss of a role model, a
strength giver, a provider, a teacher. For many daughters,
losing a father means all of that, but also losing the first and
perhaps the only man in the world who would truly love
them no matter what. The one man who would always look
at them and say with absolute honesty, "You are beautiful."

God sees your troubles, and He knows your pain.
When you come to Him in prayer, He cradles you in the
palm of His hand because He is that big. Big enough to
take on your sorrow. Big enough to lift us all. Yet close
enough and gentle enough to wipe your tears and whisper,
"You are beautiful."

*Father God, thank You for never*
*leaving me. Please hold on tight. Amen.*

# Humbled

*We all, like sheep, have gone astray, each of us has
turned to our own way; and the LORD has laid
on him the iniquity of us all.*

ISAIAH 53:6 NIV

When you come to God in prayer, do you ever feel the
complete humbleness of your situation? Perhaps that's why
we don't do it as often as we should. It's not comfortable
to feel shame.

We are sheep. We run away. We ramble. We get off
track. We lose our way. We chase after the wrong things.
We fear everything. We cry out and complain. We can't
find our way home. We are stubborn. We don't see well.
We don't ask for help. We stumble.

Our Lord and Shepherd knows all of this, and loves
us still. He knows all of our wrongs, and He doesn't just
forget them or wipe them away. He pays for them. In blood.

That is the God to whom you say your bedtime prayers.

*Dear God, I am humbled in Your presence.
Help me to live a life that is worthy of Your love. Amen.*

## *Transforming*

*And we all, who with unveiled faces contemplate
the Lord's glory, are being transformed into his
image with ever-increasing glory, which comes
from the Lord, who is the Spirit.*

2 CORINTHIANS 3:18 NIV

Thanks be to God, "where the Spirit of the Lord is, there is freedom" (v. 17). No one has to hide from the Lord. No one has to worry about the exterior image. No one has to feel alone.

If you have been running away from God for a while, or just neglecting your prayer life, it's time to turn and face Him. He does not expect you to be perfect. He expects that you will need transforming. He is happy to perform that work. He wants to shape you into the best human being you can be. Come and kneel before Him; don't hide your face. He can see through any veil you might try to wear anyway. Come and stand before His image and ask Him to transform you.

*Dear God, I'm not happy with who I am.
Please mold me into the person You
want me to be. Amen.*

# When Prayer Seems Impossible

*LORD, save us! LORD, grant us success! Blessed is he
who comes in the name of the LORD. From the
house of the LORD we bless you.*
PSALM 118:25–26 NIV

Sometimes the last thing we feel like doing is praying.

We're angry. We're scared. We're exhausted, we're
world weary.

Maybe we feel as though our prayers are never heard.
That we are truly alone. That life seems hopeless.

What in the world do we do? Pray.

Yes, even then. The book of Psalms is full of every
manner of heart-cry to the Almighty. Nothing is held
back. Every tear is shed in those passages. Every weary
thought is revealed. Every doubt and misery expressed.
And what happened? God listened. He came near. He
became the people's rescuer and redeemer. As in Bible
times, God may not choose to lift us out of every storm,
but when we cry out, He will be there with us, whether
it's in a howling gale or still blue sea.

*Savior, please be with me in my hour
of need and bring me hope. Amen.*

# How Beautiful Is Thy Name!

*All flocks and herds, and the animals of the wild,
the birds in the sky, and the fish in the sea. . .Lord,
our Lord, how majestic is your name in all the earth!*
<small>PSALM 8:7–9 NIV</small>

When we experience an alpine walk along a misty trail, or take in the moon's reflection on a still blue sea; when we hear the thunderous roar of a lion, or the voice of the wind through swaying palms: Don't we feel a sweet ache in our hearts to be thankful—to Someone?

God's creation is indeed full of beauty and wonder, and we should take great pleasure in His handiwork. We should explore His world. We should see with new eyes each morning.

As Christians we do not worship creation, but we instead worship the One who is the Creator of such magnificence. A thankful heart full of praise is a form of prayer. Shall we thank Him and praise Him today?

Lord, our Lord, how majestic is Your name in all the earth!

*Creator God, thank You for the beauty and wonder
of Your handiwork. Give me grateful eyes
to see it every day. Amen.*

# Words Gone Bad

*May these words of my mouth and this meditation
of my heart be pleasing in your sight, LORD,
my Rock and my Redeemer.*
**PSALM 19:14 NIV**

Once our words are spoken, once they have tumbled out of our mouths, we can never get them back. They are like the water that plunges from a cliff into the sea. It just keeps on going, flowing and changing everything it touches. That water cannot come back. Our words cannot come back into our mouths. Yes, we can apologize and make amends. We can ask the Lord to forgive us, and He will keep His promise. Yet the sting of those thoughtless remarks can sometimes last a lifetime—in the recipient's heart as well as in our own spirits.

A helpful daily prayer would be to ask the Lord to temper our words with wisdom and love. That what we say will not go bad like a rotten piece of fruit, but that our words will be pleasing and good and usable in His sight!

*God, help my words to always be kind,
compassionate, and uplifting. Amen.*

# He Holds the Blueprint

*"And even the very hairs of your
head are all numbered."*
MATTHEW 10:30 NIV

We each are uniquely and wonderfully made. It is our loving Creator who holds that blueprint—which He considers precious—that has your name on it.

Imagine God so loving the world—loving us—that His "knowing" extends to the number of hairs on our heads. He knows every single thing about us. The kind of friends we enjoy. Our favorite ice cream, favorite pets, and favorite hobbies. The things that tickle our funny bones. The things that make us cry at the movies. Every secret we've hidden. Our deepest longings. Our worst nightmares. Yes, the Lord knows every nuance and detail about us. He loves us dearly.

Knowing these truths will help us to pray, since being loved and understood by the One to whom we are praying makes all the difference in the way we begin: "Dear Lord. . ."

*Thank You for knowing and loving every single part
of me. Help me to run to You when I feel
misunderstood or forgotten. Amen.*

# His Ways

*Therefore, in order to keep me from becoming conceited,
I was given a thorn in my flesh, a messenger of Satan,
to torment me. Three times I pleaded with the Lord to take
it away from me. But he said to me, "My grace is sufficient
for you, for my power is made perfect in weakness."*

2 CORINTHIANS 12:7–9 NIV

This is a biblical concept that is puzzling, since weakness in a world that values strength seems unacceptable. But God's ways are not our ways—and this truth in tension, as one might call it, is His divine view of our struggles, not ours.

Perhaps we could ask this—what if our weakness forces us to slow down and hear God more clearly? What if that struggle gives us more compassion for others? What if that frailty is made perfect as it illuminates God's power rather than drawing attention to man's efforts? This might help us to understand that thorn—even the one that aches in our own flesh.

*God, when I am weak and afflicted, give me
Your strength. Apart from You I am nothing. Amen.*

## Better to Endure

*"He cuts off every branch in me that bears no fruit,
while every branch that does bear fruit he prunes
so that it will be even more fruitful."*
JOHN 15:2 NIV

How many times have we met children who haven't been disciplined by their parents, who've been given whatever they wanted, whenever they wanted, without any sensitivity to what they really needed? Not a pretty sight. Later, they end up being such miserable adults that they may even miss out on what they were destined to be.

The Lord wants the best for each of us—and the best sometimes requires that uncomfortable d-word. Discipline. But wouldn't it be better to endure God's occasional pruning than the devil's persuasions and praise? The Lord wants more for us than we can even imagine for ourselves.

Thank God today for His corrections, for they are full of mercy and love.

They are beautiful.

*Dear Lord, thank You for always desiring what is best
for me, even if it sometimes requires painful discipline.
Help me to trust Your sovereignty and love. Amen.*

# When We Think of God

*For you make me glad by your deeds, LORD; I sing for joy
at what your hands have done. How great are your
works, LORD, how profound your thoughts!*
PSALM 92:4–5 NIV

There is nothing about God and His creation that is
humdrum. Nothing. He made the elegant silhouette of a
swan. The shimmer of a sunrise on a pristine glacier. The
whispers of tropical wildlife still unknown to man.

When we think of God and His creation, our words
should be transformed. They might become: Mysterious.
Exotic. Breathtaking. Radiant. Exhilarating. Enlivening.
Miraculous. Prayer is connecting with that mind. That
heart. That brilliance. That life and color. That perfection.

Let us come into His presence with thanksgiving and
praise. Let us come to know Him who is extraordinary
beyond compare. And through that communion, let us
see His world and His people as they were meant to be.

*Creator God, open my eyes to the richness and vibrancy of
life. I want to encounter each day with the freedom and
joy that is abundant in a relationship with You. Amen.*

# Spa Day for the Soul

*One of those days Jesus went out to a mountainside*
*to pray, and spent the night praying to God.*
LUKE 6:12 NIV

What about having a spa day for the soul? Talk about rejuvenating. We would come away with a new outlook, a smile on our lips, and a song in our hearts. Our spirits might even feel ten years younger.

When Jesus walked among us, He showed us how important prayer was. It says in God's Word that Christ went out to the mountainside to pray and spent the night praying to God. He knew how powerful and vital prayer was, and how He needed it to stay the course.

So are you ready to schedule a spa day for your soul? A day of prayer and communion with your Lord? Or even an hour on Sunday? The luxury of this refreshment is gratis, and its beautification will be a lift to the body and spirit.

*Lord, help me to remember to regularly refresh*
*my spirit through prayer. My soul needs You as*
*much as my body needs oxygen. Amen.*

# The Hardest Prayer

*Going a little farther, he fell with his face to the ground
and prayed, "My Father, if it is possible, may this cup
be taken from me. Yet not as I will, but as you will."*
MATTHEW 26:39 NIV

When we pray, asking God for help, we have a good idea
of what we need.

Yet we don't. We can't possibly know. So, when we
pray, we should end our petitions with, "Your will be
done." Hmmm. It means we'd have to trust God for our
every need. All the time. Night and day. Do we really trust
Him that much?

Even Jesus, on the night before His crucifixion, when
He knew He would be betrayed by His followers and die a
brutal death on the cross, still ended His prayer with "Your
will be done." Yes, Jesus did ask God for a way out—in
other words, was there another way for redemption to come
to man other than His death on the cross? In fact, Christ
asked God this question three times. But in the end, our
Lord said the words "Your will be done."

Jesus trusted. And so should we.

*God, even when I am discouraged and afraid, help me to
trust in Your will for my life. You know what's best. Amen.*

# Meet, Pray, Love

*Dear children, let us not love with words or speech but with actions and in truth.*
1 JOHN 3:18 NIV

Sometimes it is true that that action involves words *and* speech. You can love someone through prayer. At times the most loving thing you can do for a person is pray with them and for them. When a person is deep in grief, holding their hands and praying with them for comfort is worth a whole shop full of flowers. When a person is stuck in depression, seeking them out and thanking God for them can be better than any other act. When a person is anxious, a walk out in the fresh air with a friend and a request to God for calm and assurance can be just exactly what the doctor ordered.

Love with actions. But love with words and speech too. And do all of it in truth.

*Dear God, help me to have courage to pray with others. Amen.*

# Call to Me

---

*"Call to me and I will answer you and tell you great and unsearchable things you do not know."*
JEREMIAH 33:3 NIV

This relationship with God, this closeness, is reflected again and again in scripture. It's there in Abraham staring at the stars, it's there in Moses on the mountain, and it's there in Mary's womb. God wants us to know, to be certain of the fact that He is with us, in us, through us.

God wants more from us than a Q and A session. He wants a constant conversation. He wants more than what we might "ask Siri." He wants to know the deepest questions of our souls—the ones that keep us up at night or frighten us with their proportions.

Oswald Chambers said in *My Utmost for His Highest*, "We look upon prayer simply as a means of getting things for ourselves, but the biblical purpose of prayer is that we may get to know God Himself."

*Dear Lord, thank You for the chance to know You more. Amen.*

## Like an Eagle

*Like an eagle that stirs up its nest and hovers*
*over its young. . . The LORD alone led him.*
DEUTERONOMY 32:11–12 NIV

God is big and unsearchable in many ways. Yet He lets us know Him and learn about Him. God is a whispering voice in our souls and yet His Word shouts truth.

God is huge and grand and impossible to fathom. He is our Father—deliverer of justice, ruler of peace, rescuer and redeemer.

God is like the eagle, which nurtures its eggs, turning them over at just the right time and keeping them at just the right temperature for proper growth. God is like the eagle, which protects its young chicks, covering them with its wings. God is like the eagle, playing with its young, letting them take chances and then always being there to catch them when they fall.

God is like the eagle, teaching us to fly, and carrying us high over the hard parts.

This is the God we call on when we pray.

*Dear God, thank You for Your tender,*
*caring love. Amen.*

# Friend and Intercessor

❧

*"My intercessor is my friend
as my eyes pour out tears to God."*
**JOB 16:20 NIV**

We have a better friend and comforter than any person we could find on earth. We have Jesus. Jesus is always there for us. Jesus speaks to God on our behalf. Can we imagine a better person to stand up for us? Jesus "pleads with God as one pleads for a friend" (v. 21).

And what does He plead? When we repent of our sins, He pleads for our forgiveness. When we have been hurt, He pleads for our restoration. When we stand before God to be judged for our worth, He stands in for us and says, "I make this one worthy."

It is good to have friends in high places. It's better still to have a friend willing to bring us up with Him.

*Dear Jesus, thank You for pleading for me. Amen.*

# My Soul to Keep

*"Let the little children come to me, and do not hinder them,
for the kingdom of God belongs to such as these."*

MARK 10:14 NIV

Some of the best prayers you will ever hear may come from the lips of a child. Children speak to God as if they were speaking to their teacher or their grandpa or their dog, Fido. They use the words that come naturally to them and don't try to sound fancy or serious.

Children will pray prayers about the ridiculous and the sublime all at the same time, sometimes even in the same breath. They have no boundaries between them and their Father, no walls to break down, no veils to hide behind.

It is no wonder that Jesus asked for the little children to be allowed to come to Him. How refreshing it must be for God to hear the prayers of hearts and minds that have not yet been made world weary. We might do well to shed our grown-up manners once in a while and pray with the children: "Now I lay me down to sleep, I pray the Lord my soul to keep."

*Dear Father, remind me that I am Your child still. Amen.*

# Quenchable

---

*"In your anger do not sin."*
**EPHESIANS 4:26 NIV**

If you know you have a temper (or even if you're sure you don't), the one way to grow stronger in restraining your anger is to pray regularly. Pray for self-control and patience. Pray for understanding and perspective, so you can stop minor irritations from growing into something harder to tame. Pray for the simple ability to just keep your mouth shut. Start with physical control, then work up to calming your thoughts and emotions. Ask God to remind you to use anger-management strategies—to walk away, to breathe deeply, to count to ten.

Pray hard. Do whatever it takes to keep your anger from becoming a fire you cannot control—to keep it from hurting others or yourself. Ask God for forgiveness when you mess up, and ask Him to teach you to forgive others.

Don't let a spark destroy your whole household.

*Dear God, help me to control*
*my mind and my mouth. Amen.*

# Praying for the Gospel

*Join with me in suffering for the gospel,*
*by the power of God.*
2 TIMOTHY 1:8 NIV

You may not be called to spread the Gospel in another language in a country far away. Yet you can help those who are. You can pray for them. You can ask God for their protection. You can ask God to give them courage and boldness. You can ask God to give them wisdom—to know when to speak and when not to, when to stand out and when to blend in.

Though you may not be called to deliver the Gospel in foreign lands, you may be surprised to find yourself an ambassador for God in your own community. Just because a place is blessed with a church on every block does not necessarily mean all its residents understand the message of love and grace that the Gospel carries with it.

Pray for an opportunity, every day, to share the Gospel or to support those who do.

*Dear Lord, help me to spread Your*
*good news around the world. Amen.*

# You Are Never Alone

*He took Peter and the two sons of Zebedee along with him,
and he began to be sorrowful and troubled. Then he said
to them, "My soul is overwhelmed with sorrow to the
point of death. Stay here and keep watch with me."*
MATTHEW 26:37–38 NIV

Jesus grew up here on earth, and He must have known many of the usual trials and triumphs of childhood. Yet when He became a man and faced His divine destiny, Christ knew the black flood of suffering—pain and anguish we cannot even imagine. He said, "My soul is overwhelmed with sorrow to the point of death." Jesus' agony was so very great, He sweat drops of blood.

When despair comes to us, be comforted in the knowledge that Jesus knows torment as deep and lonely as the darkest reaches of hell. In your hour of need, He will hold you in the palm of His hand, because He understands like no one else. Because He loves you. He always has loved you—enough to die for you.

When you pray—know this truth—you are never ever alone in that dark night.

*Father, in times of despair, shield and sustain me.
Be my source of comfort. Amen.*

# Those Who Bring Good News

*How, then, can they call on the one they have not believed in? And how can they believe in the one of whom they have not heard? And how can they hear without someone preaching to them? And how can anyone preach unless they are sent? As it is written: "How beautiful are the feet of those who bring good news!"*
ROMANS 10:14–15 NIV

When God created earth, He did ask us to be good stewards of His beautiful world, but over the years our priorities have shifted; we now focus more on the needs of our planet than on the needs of people and their souls.

As Christians, when we leave this earth and come to meet our Maker face to face, He won't be as concerned about whether we recycled as much as whether we obeyed His mandate of sharing the Gospel. Did we spend our days worrying about our carbon footprint or more of our time dealing with the eternal imprint that we were able to leave by sharing the good news of Christ?

Let us always pray for opportunities to share the mercy and love of our Savior with people of all nations—whether it's overseas or simply across the street.

*Lord, remind me of my calling as a Christian.*
*Give me the boldness to carry out Your plan. Amen.*

# The Heart That Chooses Joy

*Rejoice in the Lord always.*
*I will say it again: Rejoice!*
PHILIPPIANS 4:4 NIV

You spilled coffee on your new dress. Your hair isn't cooperating. It never does. Your friend canceled lunch—again. On top of that, you're afraid to tell your spouse that you dropped your cell phone in the mud. When you finally get home, you just want to be left alone on the couch to vegetate. Right?

Yet God says rejoice. We are not expected to celebrate the unhappy circumstances in life, but we can have joy in the midst of them. Try picking ten things in your life that you're grateful for, and then during your prayer time, rejoice in your heart by thanking God for these blessings. Thank Him for His goodness. His gift of eternal life. His faithfulness. His mercies are new every morning.

A soul filled with the world's mind-set will wilt, but a heart that chooses holy joy will look up, and it will be renewed.

*Father, help me to think on Your goodness and*
*provision instead of my worries and frustrations.*
*Thank You for Your love, mercy, and patience. Amen.*

# Gentle and Humble of Heart

*God chose the lowly things of this world and
the despised things—and the things that
are not—to nullify the things that are.*

1 Corinthians 1:28 niv

Throughout the Bible, we see God selecting people for His tasks who might be considered by the world's standards to be very unwise choices. Yet God does not see people the way we see them. He may pick someone—whom the world despises because of a lack of wealth or fame or academic accolades or clever wit or worldly savvy—and raise her up to show a haughty society just how foolish their pride looks.

The Gospel of Matthew says, "Blessed are the meek, for they will inherit the earth" (5:5 niv). Jesus called himself gentle and humble of heart. So, if you are feeling unfit for duty because you are humble and lowly by the world's standards, take heart. God loves the meek. If you feel you are lacking in a gentle and selfless spirit, just ask God for one, and He would be pleased to give it to you.

*Father, thank You for loving misfits, outcasts,
and sinners. Cultivate in me a spirit of humility. Amen.*

## Expectation

*"Ask and it will be given to you; seek and you will find; knock and the door will be opened to you. For everyone who asks receives; the one who seeks finds; and to the one who knocks, the door will be opened."*

MATTHEW 7:7–8 NIV

When we call on the Lord for help and mercy, we can come into His presence with expectation. In His Word He promises to hear our prayers, to open the door to us, to give us what we need. The Gospel of Matthew goes on to say, "Which of you, if your son asks for bread, will give him a stone? Or if he asks for a fish, will give him a snake? If you, then, though you are evil, know how to give good gifts to your children, how much more will your Father in heaven give good gifts to those who ask him!" (vv. 9–11).

Of course, the gifts that the Lord chooses to give us might be wisdom or forgiveness or peace or joy. These gifts may not be material, but they are timeless. So, like a child on her birthday, come to Christ with anticipation of good things, of delight, and wonder!

*Father, thank You for all of the wonderful gifts You've given me. I have hope in Your loving provision. Amen.*

# A Tree Planted by the Water

*"But blessed is the one who trusts in the LORD.... They will
be like a tree planted by the water that sends out its roots
by the stream. It does not fear when heat comes; its leaves
are always green. It has no worries in a year
of drought and never fails to bear fruit."*
JEREMIAH 17:7–8 NIV

The streams have dried up. The land is barren. Rain is only
a memory. The cicadas may be the only thing left singing.
Have you ever experienced this kind of serious drought?
If you have, it is unforgettable. Drought is a brutal force
of nature—an unforgiving taskmaster. That is the way of
the world. It will steal your strength until you are weak
and vulnerable and fruitless.

Yet prayer can build up our trust in the Lord. He is our
strength in a harsh and desolate land. If we faithfully spend
time with Him and His good Word, we will be like that
tree in the book of Jeremiah. We will be that tree planted
by the water that sends out its roots by the stream. A tree
that does not fear the heat or a year of drought. It's the
kind of tree that will never fail to bear fruit.

*Lord, when I'm feeling dried up, give me the strength
to turn to You with outstretched arms. Amen.*

# Hope Arrived One Night

*The Word became flesh and made his dwelling among us.*
*We have seen his glory, the glory of the one and only Son,*
*who came from the Father, full of grace and truth.*
JOHN 1:14 NIV

Because of our Creator's love for us, hope arrived one night in a small bundle in a lowly place—a baby whose name was Immanuel, which in Hebrew means, "God is with us." Yes, it was a simple birth, but it was also grace filled. It was a sacred night that would change the course of human history.

JESUS: He is the only hope this broken world has ever known. The book of Isaiah tells us, "And he will be called Wonderful Counselor, Mighty God, Everlasting Father, Prince of Peace" (Isaiah 9:6 NIV). What a mighty Savior. What hope everlasting!

The nativity scene and the empty tomb should become more to us than mere historical highlights and entertaining holidays. Let them become truths that transform our minds and hearts—not just once a year during Christmas, but every day. In every prayer.

*Jesus, thank You for making Yourself poor by coming down to earth so that I could be made rich by Your grace. Amen.*

# The Season of Singing

*"See! The winter is past; the rains are over and gone.
Flowers appear on the earth; the season of singing
has come, the cooing of doves is heard in our land."*
**SONG OF SONGS 2:11–12 NIV**

Is your life caught up in a cold winter that never seems to end? Then snuggle up in a warm blanket of truth.

God provides you with His mighty Word to heat and stir your soul. He offers you the safe and sheltering knowledge of eternal life through Christ. Under the lamp of these truths we can sing in our hearts, knowing spring is near.

In time, the cold will go. The ice will thaw. The rain will cease and the sun will burst boldly through the clouds in rays of pure gold. The earth will turn a lush green, and flowers will spring up in a profusion of color. Even the gentle cooing of doves will be heard all through the land. What beauty. What hope. What joy.

*God, give me joy and patience in the long winters
of life. Remind me of Your steadfast presence and
may Your Word strengthen and comfort me. Amen.*

# Grabber Hogs

*For although they knew God, they neither glorified him as God nor gave thanks to him, but their thinking became futile and their foolish hearts were darkened.*

ROMANS 1:21 NIV

The Bible clearly tells us that we can make our requests known to God. He cares very much for our needs. And yet, there is more to prayer than the material world and what we want right now. There is thanksgiving, praise, repentance, praying for the needs of others; there is listening to that still, small voice for knowledge and guidance, for peace and for strength for the day. And there is tender communion.

Ask Him for a change in our heart's desires—that they will be aligned with His—and the need to have it all will be replaced with something more lasting, more treasured. Doesn't the word "contentment" have a sweeter feel to it than the world's "grabber hog" philosophy?

*Father, forgive me for neglecting to thank You for all that You've given me. Give me a spirit of contentment, that I might praise and thank You in all circumstances. Amen.*

# New Every Morning

*Because of the LORD's great love we are not consumed,*
*for his compassions never fail. They are new every*
*morning... I say to myself, "The LORD is my*
*portion; therefore I will wait for him."*
LAMENTATIONS 3:22–24 NIV

A crisp new linen tablecloth whipped up in the air and smoothed down just right for the arrival of one's guests. A snowfall that covers over a dingy landscape, transforming it into pristine and dazzling loveliness... Such beauty and promise is in all things new.

The old is past. The new has come. Oh, how that inspires us. The Lord promises that His compassions never fail. They are new every morning. He assures us that His faithfulness is beyond the ordinary—it's extraordinary!

What can we do in this new dawn that will help celebrate this fresh start? An apology to someone we've wronged? Connecting with someone who feels lost? Extending forgiveness to others and to ourselves? A helping hand? Or perhaps quiet time spent with the Savior who wants to make your heart new and your soul refreshed again?

*Help me to wake up with a refreshed spirit, equipped to*
*encounter any storms because You are with me. Amen.*

# Scripture Index